Horses have hooves to carry them over frost and snow, and hair to protect them from wind and cold. They eat grass and drink water, and fling up their tails and gallop. Ceremonial halls and big dwellings are of no use to them. . . . When pleased, they rub their necks together. When angry, they turn round and kick up their heels at each other. Such is the real nature of horses.

—Chuangtse

SUCH IS
THE REAL NATURE
OF HORSES

ROBERT VAVRA

WILLIAM MORROW AND COMPANY, INC.

New York   1979

This book is dedicated to people who admire horses, and especially to my friend and assistant José Franco Cadena.

Planned and reproduced by Rudolf Blanckenstein & Associates

Copyright © 1979 by Robert Vavra

Library of Congress Catalog Card Number 79-52901

ISBN 0-688-03504-3
Color reproductions by Cromoarte, Barcelona, Spain
Printed in Germany
by Ernst Uhl, Radolfzell
4 5 6 7 8 9 10

Designed by John Fulton

CONTENTS

INTRODUCTION

When I was finishing some brief notes on the social behavior of horses, for possible use in the book *Equus,* I wrote to a friend, Carolyn Moyer, in California, to see if she could locate any published material on the subject. My four-month study of horses in southern Spain had been so distracted by photography that I hoped the books she might find would confirm or refute some of the conclusions I had drawn.

"I have turned the local libraries upside down, looking for material on equine social behavior," wrote Carolyn, "including the university at Davis. I've found material on literally every aspect of horses but social behavior. This is unbelievable to me. They have entire tomes on conformation, breeding, training, showing, pathology, illness—you can also get the stud books for nearly every breed of horse in the world—and even biographies of famous horses. I thought when I started the search that it would be a matter of culling out the best material for you, not desperately searching for anything on the subject. As far as published material goes you are really in *terra incognita* with this one."

Fortunately, before *Equus* went to press, Dr. Patrick Duncan, an ecologist who leads a horse-study project in southern France, visited Seville and reviewed my notes. Shortly after leaving Spain he wrote to me: "Why has the horse, inspiration of so much creative art over millennia, been so little studied except in captivity or for breeding purposes? This lack of scientific attention is particularly striking when contrasted with the abundance of excellent new work on the behavior and ecology of exotic and distant species, such as the gorilla and lion (George Schaller), elephant (Iain and Oria Douglas-Hamilton) and chimpanzee (Jane Goodall)."

Carolyn Moyer's fruitless search in California, and my own fascination with horse behavior, decided me to expand my notes and include them in *Equus*. Once the book was published, however, it seemed to me that the reader could not really get a good picture of horse behavior if he had to depend on the text alone. There seemed only one sensible way to present horse behavior: to illustrate it with many photographs. When the reader reaches the last page of this book and reflects, for example, on eye rolling, I hope that instead of the printed words on a page, memory will project in his mind a picture of a gray stallion, his head held high, with eyes completely turned so that the pupil is out of sight.

This book does not presume to reflect more than the most obvious forms of equine behavior. Patrick Duncan and his colleagues at Tour du Valat in the South of France are involved in a highly scientific study that will be of interest to readers who desire academic and technical descriptions. Perhaps one reason why books on horse behavior for the layman do not exist is the lack of locations for the study of horses in Europe and the United States, where they are of such interest to so many people. Equines must be living in herds at liberty or semi-liberty to behave as most of those that were photographed for this book. Wild horses, like the mustangs of North America, are so cagey that they make difficult subjects, although the late James D. Feist, Dale R. McCullough and Hope Ryden have made keen observations on their behavior.

I have the good fortune to spend some months each year in Spain, where horses are still kept in sizable herds, mainly by the Spanish military. Besides large herds of mares pastured together (in some cases more than 150 head), there are also groups of bachelor stallions that often held my interest for hours. Equine family units that were studied in different parts of the world include a herd of Przewalski's horses, quarter horses and Andalusians. The most explicit and vivid examples of the social behavior of horses, however, were observed in southern France in the marshes of the Camargue.

THE

HERD

A seemingly fiery stallion leading a thundering herd, the photograph on pages 8 and 9 could be a frame for a Hollywood film. In truth, however, horses living at liberty, unmolested by man, rarely gather in groups of more than a dozen. The photograph on the previous page shows an all-mare herd living in semi-liberty. The stallions I have observed in various countries usually rule harems numbering from two to eight mares and their offspring. Infrequent gatherings of several family units do take place when groups, pasturing in relatively close proximity, flee from danger. When this occurs, the dominant stallion usually brings up the rear while the other male heads of families position themselves on either side of the herd. Once the horses have outdistanced potential danger each stallion gathers his harem and the herds separate.

Photograph 2 shows nearly one hundred mares. The behavior of mares in this controlled group differs in some ways from that of wild females in natural family units. The true harem, dominated by a single stallion, is today almost nonexistent. Equines still living in these highly structured social groups are plains zebra, feral horses of North and South America and Australia, Camargue horses, the ponies of Sable Island, off Nova Scotia, a very few horses in southern Spain and

more in the north and, if they are not completely extinct, some Przewalski's horses in Mongolia. Outside these carefully guarded herds roam gangs of young bachelors not yet mature or experienced enough to beat an established stallion in battle or to take on the responsibility of one or more mares. Herd living, apart from offering the collective warning system, is especially important to breeding. With gangs of strong young bachelors roaming about, family stallions are replaced once they become too old or weak to be effective sires or to protect their harems.

While there are basic universal behavior patterns among horses living at liberty or semi-liberty, there are also differences. For example, the horses that I observed in southern Spain did not behave exactly in the same manner as did those in the Camargue. There mature females seldom engage in mutual grooming, while in Andalusia this activity seems an important part of social interaction in female herds. While the bachelors that I watched in Spain often dropped to their knees like zebra to fight, the young mustang stallions studied by James D. Feist and Dale Mc-Cullough seldom do. Both Hope Ryden and Steven W. Pellegrini have observed lead stallions in the western United States to combine their harems during the fall and winter months when mares were not in heat. During this period, one stallion dominated the other, assuming the flank position while driving the combined herd. Having witnessed in Spain the intolerance of dominant stallions in close contact with another male and his mares, I found this report difficult to believe until I saw family units living side by side in the Camargue.

The structure of social organizations among equines often varies considerably. Since most wild horses have had their home ranges manipulated by man, perhaps the only insight into the true social arrangement of the herd can be gleaned from some mustang groups or from observations of equids in Africa. Hans Klingel, in his remarkable studies, found that social organization varied markedly from species to species. Plains and mountain zebra, for example, live in coherent family groups consisting of one stallion with one or more mares and their young. Nonterritorial, these social units move freely over rather large home ranges. Mares usually spend their lifetime with the same group. On the other hand, Klingel observed that Grévy's zebra and the wild ass have completely different social organizations. These species form no permanent bonds among adult animals, and the stallions of both species are territorial. It would seem that the social organization of the free-living horse most resembles that of the plains zebra. Zebra, migrating, do gather together in herds as large as that of Arab, Thoroughbred and Andalusian mares shown in 3, but like the six-mare Przewalski harem which appears with its stallion in 4, the wild-horse family unit is usually independent and small.

3

4

HIERARCHY

One of the most social of animals, the horse maintains a well-defined hierarchy within the group. This pecking order serves a vital need by providing hard-and-fast rules for social interaction. Each horse knows his role and, as long as his situation is well defined, feels relatively secure, even though he is at the bottom of the totem pole. Herd life, even for a very subordinate, picked-on animal, offers at least the security of the protection of the lead stallion and other dominant horses against intruders and predators.

When a stallion, such as the gray in 5, joins a harem of mares, it may be days, weeks or even months before he is accepted by them. Within the all-mare herds that I studied, relationships, depending on the size of the herd, were frequently complicated. At the Spanish Army's Vicos ranch, for example, one gray mare threatened a bay, who in turn threatened a black mare. On several occasions, though, the black horse threatened the gray. Most of the mares in this herd, however, seemed aware of their own position in the hierarchy, and subordinate animals would usually avoid their superiors. In Spain the system of rank in mare herds did not appear nearly so well defined as that in bachelor groups. Stallions, being active, dominant animals, are more obvious in their threat gestures than are mares, a fact which at first causes the observer to feel that bachelor hierarchy is stronger than that of the mare herd. In truth, however, the mare hierarchy is the most permanent and defined of all. A very dominant mare has only to flick an ear or swish her tail to frighten away a subordinate.

Mare hierarchies were much more obvious in small all-female herds than in family units, where stallion dominance eclipsed other relationships. Photographed half an hour after having been turned to some mares, the gray stallion in 5 is rearing, laying back his ears, flexing his muzzle and slightly rolling his eyes in an attempt to impress his importance on two fillies who are jealously trying to guard an older sister in heat.

6

7   8

In 6 the stallion is holding his ground as the fillies, ears laid back in threat, close in to attack. The offensive begins in 7. The light-gray filly holds the stallion's attention from the front while her darker sister kicks out from the rear.

As both fillies approach from behind (8), the stallion rears in a threat display, attempting to impress them. When this fails (9), he kicks out as hard as he can. It is important that he establish the herd hierarchy as quickly as possible so that he can gather the mares into a compact social unit. When the fillies persist in defiance (10), the stallion lays back his ears, rolls his eyes, threatens to kick again and screams to scatter them and assert his dominance.

9

10

17

In spite of their size and strength, horses are timid animals, and can be sent into blind panic by the most harmless stimulus if it is unknown or comes as a surprise. It should not be forgotten that the horse is born a wild creature whose feared enemy was, and in many instances still is, man. The newborn foal's long legs are ready within a few short hours to be used for his most vital defense—flight. Animals observed in groups followed the same escape patterns, whether they were family units such as those of the Coto Doñana, the King Ranch, the ranch of Paco Lazo, or all-mare herds and bachelor groups. If the surprise or threat was overwhelming, most animals fled in panic, though dominant family stallions were never victims of flight hysteria. The bands would react quickly in the same manner, fleeing with the high-ranking mares and foals in the lead followed by the subordinate mares, the stallion always bringing up the rear. When the group consisted of mares only, the stallion's position (though not so well defined) was taken by one of the more dominant females, who snapped at the flanks of the animals in front of her. Each herd of males at Écija also had a high-ranking stallion. It appeared to me that where family groups were involved, the direction of flight was sometimes set by the lead female, usually an old mare, the stallion's duty being primarily to hurry lagging animals and to challenge pursuers.

While herd hierarchy can most clearly be seen when horses feed, drink or arrive at a dusting spot, the dominant horses showing their superiority by laying back their ears and threatening to kick and bite subordinates, who move hastily away, rank can also be determined by watching a group of animals in flight. When on the run, dominant horses often threaten subordinates who attempt to pass them.

FLIGHT

12

13

The dark horse in 12 extends its neck, lays back its ears, rolls its eyes and flexes its muzzle to warn the lighter-gray stallion, who reacts by flattening his ears and trying to keep out of reach. He is not aware of me, stretched flat on the ground along the trail, as are the two center horses, whose ears and eyes clearly show their suspicion. In 13 two chestnut stallions quarrel while the herd is in flight. Here the threatened horse, second from left, indicates that he has not been inhibited by arching his neck, rolling his eyes and flashing his teeth. As is shown in 12, a low-ranking horse, stallion or mare, will usually try to avoid a superior. Age, size and temperament, as well as inherited dominance, are the factors that most influence the herd hierarchy. On a number of occasions, though, I did see small but aggressive horses display dominance over larger, older animals.

Running horses usually lay their ears back to avoid insects and dust, as is shown in 14 (that is, except for the two stallions whose ears and eyes have discovered the photographer).

14

Eating, in terms of hours spent, is the most time-consuming activity in the life of the horse. Animals grazed the pastures where I was working for eleven to thirteen hours a day. Unlike carnivores, who can eat rapidly because of the elasticity of their stomachs, and who can subsist on relatively small amounts of food due to the high nutritive value of meat, horses must eat immense quantities of vegetation in order to maintain enough weight and strength for normal activity. The average horse consumes twenty to thirty pounds of vegetation per day, depending on the availability of food.

Because of the low nutritive value of their diet, equines have relatively long digestive tracts, requiring an extended digestive period to get the most out of every blade of grass. The horse's small intestine is seventy feet long, with a capacity of over sixty quarts, and the large colon is ten to twelve feet long, with a capacity of about eighty-five quarts. The entire alimentary canal, from mouth to anus, is one hundred feet long. The average horse excretes from twenty-five to forty pounds of feces a day, depending on its food intake.

Since their food-to-stomach process is a one-act operation, horses, unlike camels, cows and antelopes, have to mill vegetation and grain in their mouths more slowly than do their cousins. It has been calculated that a horse secretes ten gallons of saliva per day from three sets of paired glands in its mouth. Mixed with food, the saliva makes chewing and swallowing easier. The horse's teeth are enormously effective in reducing feed into finely divided particles which provide a larger surface area for the action of the digestive juices.

Stallions have forty teeth, while mares, who usually lack canines, have thirty-six. Horses use both up and down chewing action as well as lateral

FOO

18

19

17

20

(side to side) action. Since the upper jaw is wider than the lower jaw, chewing takes place on only one side of the mouth at a time. Because of the lateral chewing motion, sharp edges often form on the outside of the upper molar teeth and on the inside of the lower molars. Not only do these sharp edges interfere with chewing, causing a horse to eat slower, but they can also cut the cheek areas and the tongue. When a horse holds his head to one side while he eats or if feed falls out of his mouth as he chews, it is almost certain that he has a tooth problem. Whole grain found in manure can also indicate faulty teeth.

When fields are heavily grazed, horses often pull up grass by the roots. This not only destroys the pastures, but, where soil is sandy, quartz taken in with roots causes noticeable premature wearing away of teeth. One twenty-year-old mare, who had passed most of her life feeding in such sandy fields near Cordoba, had teeth which had been worn down practically to stumps. When grass is exhausted, horses sometimes paw the soil away from taproots, which then are either bitten off or pulled out of the ground and eaten. Hooves are also used to remove snow from grass and ice from water.

At the Urquijo ranch in southern Spain, the first time I really paid close attention to the way horses ate, I was amazed at how adept they were at selecting and plucking individual grasses. Although springtime had filled the pastures with a variety of plants, herd members were quite choosy in what they ate; some were more selective than others. I was fascinated to watch such large animals accept one fragile plant while at the same time rejecting another. The horse is able to accomplish this delicate selection because of its prehensile upper lip, which is not only strong and mobile but also extremely sensitive. The tongue rejects unwanted materials by forcing them out of the side of the mouth.

Commenting on the selectivity with which his Camargue horses ate, Patrick Duncan wrote:

"Much of our effort has gone into studies of feeding, by which horses modify their environment most. Observation throughout the year is showing us some of the ways in which selection of habitat and diet, and the time of grazing, are modified in response to the sharp seasonal changes which occur; experimental enclosures provide quantitative data on how the vegetation would be were there no horses. You have pointed out that Andalusian horses can feed very selectively; in the Camargue, we have found not only that horses feed very selectively, but also their selectivity changes dramatically from one season to another. For example, they feed intensively on reeds in spring and summer, but ignore them completely in winter."

During the spring, there is such a paradise of greenery everywhere in Andalusia that most mares seem to suffer from food mania, bulging their bellies to immense proportions, storing fat that will help them survive the harsh, barren summer months when temperatures in the shade often reach 111° F. When the marshes of the Guadalquivir River and of the Rhone were flooded in winter, I was intrigued to watch herd members grazing with their muzzles below the water, something I would have thought impossible for them to do. On a number of occasions when grass was scarce, food envy manifested itself as one mare threatened another—gesturing or lunging at her. In spite of this the distance between animals never became so great as to dissolve the herd.

James D. Feist and Dale R. McCullough report that when food became scarce, the mustangs they were watching supplemented their diet by eating old feces. They saw mature, immature and yearling mares eating from a stallion fecal pile. These observations, they continued, did not agree with reports that adult wild horses reject the feces of other equines, but that foals do consume the fresh feces of their dams, which is thought to ensure acquisition of the proper intestinal bacterial flora. Feist and McCullough feel that mustangs eat old feces when there is a lack of good natural forage. On another occasion, the same observers also watched a lone stallion eat mud from a nearly dried water puddle. Ungulates also obtain minerals by chewing bones and from natural salt licks.

21

22

WATER

23

Horses living at liberty in semi-arid regions generally drink once a day and usually do not range much farther than two to three miles from the water hole. In extremely hot weather, of course, they may water several times during the day and pass more time at a spring. Family units will usually spend from five to twenty minutes drinking. Marsh horses, being surrounded by water, naturally drink more often. The quantity of water drunk depends also on the active state of the horse and on the amount of salt available in its diet.

When a band approaches a water hole it usually does so in single file, with the dominant stallion or mare leading. Of the animals I studied in Andalusia, some, arriving at a pond or stream, drank immediately, others pawed at the water. Lactating mares often arrived first and drank longest.

During the final three or four months of pregnancy, when fetuses grow most, changes in the mares' drinking behavior could sometimes be noted. It seemed that

24

25

early in the morning the very heavy mares drank less. Perhaps especially cold water, if taken in large quantities, causes cramps and stimulates the movement of the unborn foal.

While the horses that I watched in southern Spain watered at no scheduled hour, but at all times during the day, feral horses and zebra, if they are disturbed, often drink only at night.

During the hot summer months in Andalusia, horses, whenever they had a chance, would roll in water or in mud left by receding ponds. I have also seen Camargue stallions roll in mud on freezing winter days.

Horses are natural swimmers, and foals can take to water, if the distance is short, when they are surprisingly young. The herd of quarter-horse mares in 24 is crossing a pond on a hot day. A lead mare is followed by three subordinates, the foals; and the group is escorted from the rear by several older females. In 23 a band of mares stands in shallow water, which not only cools them on this hot summer evening, but also helps them to avoid insects. The horses I watched in Spain also dealt with insects by seeking high ground, where breezes are strongest—and with good reason. In one day flies can suck as much as half a liter of blood from a horse. Camargue herds on the other hand frequently seek low areas where vegetation and dust are abundant, both of which offer some protection against insects. Foot-stamping, head-shaking, skin-twitching and mutual tail-swishing are also used to help shoo away flies.

26

As the mares and foals in 26 ford a pond, the two dark females in the lead have their ears pricked forward suspiciously; the foals follow their mothers. The old white mare in the rear, eyes rolling and ears laid back, urges on all the animals, and seems especially concerned with the younger ones. As the group emerges from the water (27), she extends her neck and nips at one of the foals to hurry it along. Since horses are especially vulnerable in the water, swimming herd members depend more than ever on the guidance of the lead stallion or mare.

Head and body signals are the forms of communication most used among horses at liberty, though smell is also important. Generally only when distance or obstacles make it impossible for animals to read these silent messages do they rely entirely on voice.

The most important and easily read signals are flagged by the ears, which provide a virtual barometer for determining a fellow herd member's moods. Positions can range from sharply forward-pointed ears, indicating tension, curiosity and good intentions; to laterally flapped-out ears, which if relaxed show boredom or fatigue but indicate anger if they are tense; to ears that are pressed flat against the mane in a warning of massive aggression. Between the extreme positions lies a whole range of subtle signals, all probably easily understood by equines. Combinations of positions are used, often in moments of anxiety or uncertainty. The ears also provide a finer means of communication, one animal receiving a message about the location of a sound stimulus by glancing at the aperture position of a fellow horse's ears. After days of observation it also seemed that equines frequently determine the wind's direction with their ears—by sound—and not only by smell.

Next to ear positions, facial expressions are probably the most important visual signals used in animal-to-animal communication. So subtle they were often hardly distinguishable, nostril flaring, muzzle wrinkling and jaw flexing played an important part in the expressions of the horses photographed. The sticking-out or tightening of the lips, the angle of curve at the edges of the mouth, and the number of teeth shown were everyday means of mute communication among herd members. The horse's ability to perceive even the slightest movements allows him to read signals that are generally indiscernible to the human eye.

Obviously, animals must be in fairly close proximity in order to employ these forms of visual language. The use of signals, however, did not seem to vary among the equines I observed.

Although mares appear not to use their eyes as much in expressing feelings as stallions do, Claudia Feh of the Tour du Valat horse-behavior study group told me that she feels female eye signals are just as frequent but are subtler and harder for the human observer to detect. Blinking or closing the eye, depending on the degree of aperture, can serve as a show of passiveness to an outside stimulus. Stallions, however, use their eyes constantly, especially while displaying.

The white stallion (28) playfully nips at a friend. His nonaggressive intentions are shown by his relaxed eye and facial muscles and by the lateral position of his

SILENT

SIGNALS

Ears back, eyes rolled, nostrils flared, the bay stallion in 34 rears to lunge at his opponent, his lips distorted to expose his teeth as he voices a shrill battle squeal. The white horse (35) leisurely stretches his neck, relaxes his mouth and nostrils, and rolls his eyes in delight as he rubs his shoulder against a tree. At such a moment of ecstasy a horse's upper lip is usually extended. Responding to an attack from a superior, the young bay stallion in 36 threatens with his mouth, opens his eyes widely, but shows subordination by not fully accepting the challenge during a play fight—he refrains from flattening his ears in a show of open aggression.

The Przewalski's mare in 37 is dozing, her head resting on another mare's neck. Her state of being can be read in her relaxed nostrils and mouth. It is much easier to read the facial messages of horses with thin skin—Arabs and Andalusians—where flexed muscles are more obvious, than of animals with thicker hides and longer coats, like the Przewalski's and Camargue horses. Suspicion and surprise flash on the face of this old white stallion (38), who, having been on the run, stops suddenly when a strange shape close to the ground catches his attention. His mood is telegraphed by his ears, tilted forward, searching for sound. Curiosity and apprehension are shown by the fixed expression of his eyes.

35

36

37

38

41

42

Nostrils flared, the two young stallions in 39 curiously sniff at one another before a play fight. The black horse (40) shows slight threat by laying back his ears and barely exposing his teeth while the bay flashes peaceful intentions with his ear position and uneasiness by his wide-open eyes. As the black increases his threat (41), the subordinate bay rears slightly in defense to show his discomfort. The black horse (42) responds by rearing and squealing while the bay maintains his defensive attitude. In 43 the black horse has followed the bay, who has run off some distance hoping to escape and whose face shows continued discomfort. The black horse (44) then turns to a chestnut stallion, who playfully accepts the challenge.

43

44

The gray stallion in 45 does not want to play-fight, and is being attacked by a black horse who wrinkles and flexes his muzzle, showing his teeth, rolls his eyes and starts to flatten his ears. The gray reveals his fear by raising his head high, tightening his lips to show his teeth while flaring eyes and nostrils.

46

One mild threat gesture, used mostly by young males, bears a resemblance to flehmen, in which a horse raises its head, wrinkles its nostrils and curls its lip up to expose its teeth (see page 71).

In 46 the black, not easily discouraged, bites at the loose skin of the subordinate stallion's neck, causing the gray to roll his eyes and scream in pain, but indicate good intentions with his ears.

Body signals are more obvious forms of communication. An outstretched neck, accompanied by ears laid back and head swung to the side, is a common threat gesture. A horse usually threatens to kick by hunching the back slightly and cocking either one or both rear legs. Stallions use their necks, arching them fully, to try to impress other horses. Mares adopt the sawhorse position to express sexual receptiveness. They also lift their tails for the same reason. A threatened subordinate horse will often tuck its tail between its legs, while a displaying stallion lifts his. Swished back and forth aggressively, a moving tail can mean discomfort or threat and "Warning." Herd members usually will all become alarmed if they see one horse come to the alert position: weight brought evenly onto all four feet, tail slightly raised and ears pointed forward. Shaking the head vigorously up and down is frequently an indication of inhibited aggression given by a horse who cannot decide whether to approach or flee from an unidentified intruder. I have had bands of semi-wild mares with young foals come toward me in a mass, their heads tossing, with ears laid back in an obvious expression of threat and aggression. Stallions will often shake their heads when they approach another stallion or when returning to the herd after having displayed.

45

Not long ago I was told by a Californian that his mares and geldings have vocabularies of twelve sounds, clearly understandable to him; and an Englishman has written that his horses use some thirty vocal expressions, ranging from "I want my bloody breakfast" to "Let's get the hell out of here!" These horse vocabularies are highly sophisticated in comparison to the basic vocalizations that I have heard used by free-running horses in western America, Andalusia and the Camargue: 1) the whinny, 2) the nicker, 3) the squeal, 4) the snort, 5) the sigh, 6) the blow, 7) the growl. Animals subjected to conditions imposed upon them by man are undoubtedly frustrated into becoming more articulate.

Spanish and French horses living in semi-wild conditions seldom use their voices, except for stallions who are displaying or fighting at dung piles, mares calling their young and vice versa, or herd members using the contact call. In herds inhabiting the cork groves in Spain there is more vocalization than among animals in the marsh, where there are few trees to obstruct vision. Repeated calling is therefore unnecessary to keep the herd together. Most of the horses observed seem able to recognize each other by voice. The high voices of the colts begin to change at puberty (roughly at two years), and reach their full depth at the age of two to three years. Males, having louder voices, appear more vocal than females, though they actually are not.

Marsh horses use the whinny in various circumstances, but mainly as a distance call. A mare who has become separated from her foal will whinny repeatedly. Some mares, however, do not seem as concerned with their offspring as others. Occasionally, if a mare is made anxious by the closeness of another horse to her foal, she will neigh, seemingly to attract the stallion's attention. Herd members will also whinny when approaching a stream, and if another family unit is there drinking, the newcomers will wait until they leave. James Feist and Dale McCullough report having seen five bands of mustangs each waiting patiently for the others to drink and abandon a water hole.

VOICE

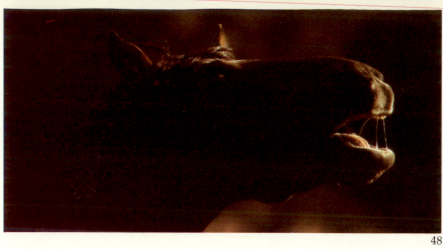

Foals who have strayed from their own group to join a harem pasturing nearby are often brought back to the home herd by their father's peremptory neigh. When two stallions spot one another, they usually neigh back and forth from some distance before approaching for mock or real battle. The imperious call of the Spanish stallions (48) is distinct from the voices of the mares around them; clearer and more penetrating, it has an unmistakable metallic tone. Some of these rolling and impressive sounds, heard most often during the spring, seem to come from the stallion's very depths.

The nicker is most often used by group members in close proximity, especially by mares and their young. Mares during courtship occasionally grind their teeth and also use soft nickers to encourage the stallion.

The squeal is heard primarily from stallions as they stand face to face during the first stage of a display or battle ritual, and accompanies the smelling of flanks as well as the kicking and biting of a real fight (50). It is also used when two males stop to smell a dung pile. Mares not in heat screech-squeal when bothered by a stallion or when trying to guard a sexually receptive sister from a male. This squeal, which starts out rather passively, can escalate into a real war cry. Mares also squeal when squabbling and kicking at one another.

The snort expresses danger and usually comes from a stallion who, once he has discovered an intruder, vocalizes and comes to the alert position. If he is deeply concerned he may take a few steps toward the intruder, stare and maybe snort again. The group members, as shown by the herd of Przewalski's (49), then gather directly behind the stallion, at which time some of them may lift their tails and defecate. If I surprised a mare who was grazing at some distance from the herd, she would generally remain silent while coming to the alert position, which would almost immediately be detected by the stallion, who would assume the same attitude and snort to warn the herd.

The sigh is probably heard as much among children playing horse as in horse herds. It is the most common of the sounds listed here. Humans imitate the sigh by blowing air out of their mouths while vibrating their lips. An expression generally of contentment, horses voice it most often while feeding, usually when clearing their nostrils.

The blow is used exclusively by stallions—an exaggerated and noisy exhalation of air from the nostrils—while displaying near a dung pile or engaged in the mock fight ritual.

Growling is used only by stallions, mostly while displaying near or on dung piles. It sounds like a very deep, chesty neigh.

49

50

H erd stallions, rarely mares, mark the excrement of other horses with their own urine or dung. Several years ago, when I first began photographing equines, I assumed that marking, as with the Grévy's zebra and the African ass, was related to territorial claims, and that even though this was an atavism it showed the twentieth-century stallion's concern to establish physical boundaries. However, more recent observations make me think that marking, so important in the life of male horses, has nothing to do with territory. If it were a behavior pattern on its way out, it would presumably not be done with the intensity and concern that stallions put into the activity.

Almost all defecation and urination by adult stallions is in relation to that of other horses: the excreta of other stallions are usually marked with dung and the excrement of mares with urine. What can be the purpose of marking? When the stallions that I watched marked mare urine, they were very particular about whose they marked. Family males paid little attention to unclaimed mares who were urinating or defecating, but they seemed to watch with great interest the harem members. Marking of mare urine was more frequent during the breeding season, and was directed mainly at the urine of older mares who were in heat or coming into heat.

It seemed that there might be two reasons for the stallion's strong preoccupation with covering only the urine of certain mares with his own. First, since horses have such a keen sense of smell, and since excreta are a means of communication among equines, a dominant male might cover a mare's urine with his own to identify her to other stallions as "personal property." Secondly, since the urine of mares in estrus or shortly before estrus contains large quantities of estrogen, the stallion, by diluting the female urine with his own, might be erasing the "I'm in heat" message left by the mare, which would attract other stallions and lead to possible conflict. The stallions I watched were obviously on the alert for urinating mares. When a

MA

51

RKING

52

dominant horse did see a mare urinate, he would move rapidly to the spot (52), smell the urine, perhaps paw the ground slightly or raise one front hoof (53), flehmen (page 71) while assuming an exaggerated stance (even more stylized in the spring) as in 51, and then mark on the mare's urine (54). He would next smell the place where both the mare and he had urinated, and flehmen. Was the second flehmen used to determine whether he had successfully erased the message left behind in the mare's urine?

On several occasions I saw stallions move rapidly to the place where a mare not in heat had just urinated, smell the spot and flehmen but refrain from marking. Once in the Camargue the dominant stallion, Darius, watched a colt smell and then flehmen over the fresh urine of a mare in estrus, after which Darius, using the direct run, attacked the young animal.

One of the first things that a stabled horse will do upon entering its cleaned box carpeted with fresh straw is to urinate, which some observers have attributed to the scent-marking of clean territory. Horses at liberty, to prevent their hocks from being splattered with urine which causes sores, also seek soft surfaces—sand or grass—and spread their legs before urinating.

Among stallions the marking of urine and dung is also used to demonstrate dominance. Subordinate stallions almost always defecate first, with dominant males following, marking the same spot in order of rank. Found mainly along well-used trails, fecal piles are often eight or more inches high and several feet in diameter. They also seem to serve as an important means of communication among horses. Few stallions can pass a dung pile without smelling it to learn if anyone was there before them, and undoubtedly they can also read from the excreta the rank of familiar horses. It seemed to me that the battles I watched started more frequently

53

54

on dung piles than on clean terrain. When two stallions arrived at a pile there was usually much posturing and gesturing (55), and then a king-of-the-mountain game was sure to ensue, with one horse proving its dominance over the other.

Defecation is also related to stress. Both mares and stallions frequently defecate before fleeing from danger, and male horses, if slightly alarmed, often stop to excrete at dung piles. The dung pile ritual, as described on page 204, was among the most interesting examples of horse behavior that I witnessed.

55

THE HAREM

M ost free-living stallions have few females in their family units. None of the semi-wild stallions that I studied ruled over a dozen mares, as each of the three King Ranch stallions at Los Millares did, let alone had to contend with thirty females as Paco Lazo's stallion did.

As a mare warns that she may kick (62) by screeching, arching her neck, hunching her rump and swishing her tail, the stallion, experienced in such matters and having previously gauged the reach of her hind hooves, steps aside, his head swinging in a high arc to avoid punishment.

The chests of most free stallions are marked with scars from mares' hooves. The white horse in 63, trying to move his harem, lunges forward, ears laid back, to bite at an obstinate white female who also flattens her ears in response, arching her body to kick. In 64 the mare, still on the move, strikes out, violently catching the stallion on the chest and throwing him off balance.

Horses relate to one another according to their personalities. A stallion who shows affection and concern for one member of his harem may constantly squabble with another. In a family unit including a number of mature females the dominant male will generally be consistent in showing most concern for his favorite mare. An inexperienced horse who is finally able to establish a harem is often henpecked by the oldest and most dominant of his females. Such a mare will threaten and literally chase a young stallion from choice feeding and watering spots.

When a free-running stallion discovers a mare in heat he usually approaches from the front, posturing: ears forward, neck arched, eyes and nostrils flared. The two will meet almost head on, the stallion positioning himself just off to one side of the mare's chest, out of striking range of her forefeet. The touching of noses is accompanied by noisy sniffing and often by squealing.

The stallion in 65 is driving one of his harem members in heat back toward the herd and away from a rival stallion. With his lips tightly pursed, ears laid back and neck extended, the lateral snake- or fishlike wobble of his lowered head shows his excitement, and warns the mare not to stray. This driving attitude also warns off other horses. In the photograph the mare has raised her tail in sexual invitation, and

COURT

her pricked ears signal peaceful intentions. A stallion at liberty will waste no time with a mare who is not in estrus and after the first few seconds of confrontation will show little interest in her.

Does love exist between horses? Displays of affection between a stallion and his favorite mare, between mares, between bachelors, and between mares and foals are often observed. Individual horses seem to differ as widely as humans in temperament and sexual appetite. A few stallions clearly favor one mare, treating her with attentive tenderness. The herd that I studied with Patrick Duncan in the Camargue had split into three bands: a bachelor group; the G herd, a trio of physically mature stallions, only the dominant one of which mated with any of the six-mare

TSHIP

T he white mare in 70 is in heat and is trying to entice the stallion away from another mare, also in estrus, who is interfering with the courtship.

The gray stallion in 71 is still unsure of the mare he has approached. He continues to try and impress her, circling and posturing. The mare, by lifting her tail in short jerks, shows the stallion next to her that she wants to be mounted. She also uses various other visual signs to indicate her desire. Before being approached by the stallion, and while still at quite some distance from him, she began flashing: lifting her tail and then opening and closing the lips of her vulva, exposing the clitoris. Mares also frequently do this following urination. Now, alongside the stallion, she spreads her legs sawhorse fashion and urinates. Occasionally a mare will attract a stallion by using these same signals which are generally obvious signs of estrus. But when the horse approaches, instead of lifting her tail she will swish it from side to side which may indicate that she is in foal from having been covered three weeks before. If this is true and she is bred again there is a risk that her pregnancy will be interrupted.

As he begins to get an erection, the horse rears slightly further to impress the mare (72). His excitement is increased by his partner's lack of resistance, and by the five invitations she has given him: legs spread in the sawhorse position, tail slightly raised, head immobile and facing straight forward, flashing and urination. As in an earlier photograph, the mare's ears warn that though ready she does not want to be bitten hard or kicked by an overly passionate suitor.

74

In 73 a stallion, ears signaling more confidence, watches the mare's rump, anxiously trying to read the silent messages she is communicating to him.

Ears rotating, another stallion also rolls his eyes slightly as he intently studies the mare's ear positions (74). Now, in 75, he feels confident enough to begin contact foreplay by biting at her neck.

Facial contact was of great importance to most of the stallions I watched. A stallion might smell a mare's hindquarters and urine and might even flehmen (page 71) without becoming sexually excited, but once having sniffed at the mare's muzzle and both horses having squealed, he would start to get an erection. The more the stallion nibbles and bites at a mare's face and neck the more excited he becomes, gradually working his way back to her hindquarters as she assumes an exaggerated sawhorse position and urinates.

75

F

Flehmen is an olfactory process used by ungulate males probably to test a female's urine to determine if she is in heat. The stallion in 79, after having smelled a mare's urine, raises his neck and head high into the air while he curls his top lip upward and slightly compresses it from the sides, shortening the distance between his nostrils. Though his teeth are exposed, his jaw remains closed. His ears are pointed forward (often also pointed outward at this moment) and his eyes are flared (in flehmen they can also be closed). The pulling back of the horse's upper lip probably brings into play an accessory olfactory zone called Jacobson's organ, whose entrance ducts are in the roof of the mouth. A mare's urine, while she is in heat, contains a high percentage of estrogen and it may be this that the stallion is trying to detect.

Although I rarely saw mares flehmen, Andalusian foals tested both their mother's and other mares' vulvas or urine in this way. A half-hour-old foal in the Camargue even flehmened when it smelled its afterbirth. Stallions also flehmen

LEHMEN

80

when they sniff a mare's dung, when they smell fecal piles, and after sniffing at their own urine. Strange, strong smells, such as cigarette smoke, may also cause a horse to flehmen.

While the stallion in 80 tests a mare, she lifts her tail. Next, in 81, as she nibbles at him, he flehmens and gets an erection. In 82 the stallion closes his eyes, positions his ears laterally, and shows his teeth but keeps his jaw firmly shut. The white stallion in 83 has just smelled fresh mare's urine after which he flehmens and urinates on the same spot. He then flehmened again six times in succession.

In 84 the muzzle position, wrinkling and flexing of the nostrils, can easily be seen. Perhaps the curled-back upper lip also causes the traces of mare smell on the stallion's nostrils to be bounced (much like blowing one's breath against one's hand) back into his nostrils, allowing him to analyze the scent more accurately.

84

81

82

83

MATING

90

Some domestic horses (90) acquire the bad habit of rearing and springing from a considerable distance onto a female's back, which, besides making entry difficult, can frighten mares, especially virgins.

The horse in 91 is about to sink his teeth into his mare's neck, which caused her to rear and kick out at him. In controlled breeding, great care should be taken not to give a virgin mare to such a rough horse. A bad first experience might make future matings difficult. A young mare is also often frightened simply when the stallion rears up behind her for the first time.

The gray horse (92) has mounted the mare from the side and although the tense expression on his face looks fierce it merely shows frustration. A half-second after this photograph was taken the stallion had the mare's ear in his mouth and was nibbling it.

In 93 the white stallion has problems—two mares in heat at the same time. While he tries to mount the younger mare the old one, who was jealous and possessive, pushes against them, her ears and eyes revealing ill intent. Earlier in the day, as the stallion copulated with the young female, the old one had bumped against them with such force that the younger mare had been knocked flat on the ground.

The gray stallion in 94, having ejaculated, remains relaxed on top of the mare.

91

92

93

94

79

BIRTH

At the end of a gestation period which lasts from 320 to 355 days, mares usually give birth in the quiet hours after midnight. As well as being the stillest hours of darkness, which must help the mare relax, most herds engage in synchronized resting during the two hours that precede dawn. For the mare in labor, whose birth fluids attract other horses, especially young males, the safety of her foal from the hooves of herd members is likely to be more assured if birth takes place at an hour when all the other horses are dozing, resting or sleeping. Birth at this time also means that she and her offspring would not be left behind by a traveling herd. Mustangs are reported to leave the harem to find a secluded spot to drop their foals, usually staying away for a day or two. Apparently this is the one time when a mustang mare is left alone and is free of the stallion's domination.

As the fetuses grow inside them, most mares show marked increase of appetite. This was especially apparent to me recently in the Camargue, as I watched, with more than casual interest, a gray mare called One Eye, who was heavy with foal. When born, would her offspring disappear? Would a stallion kill it? Not one of the three foals dropped so far in 1978 had survived. One had disappeared; one had drowned; one had been trampled. And as One Eye's pregnancy ended, it was decided that she should be watched twenty-four hours a day. Patrick Duncan, Claudia Feh, Jean Claude Gleize, Peter Paalvast, and Phil Malkas, who comprise the horse study group, watched the mare during the long, cold hours of night, through rain and snow, and since I was in the field with the horses from dawn until dusk I watched her then. There were hours when the rain fell so hard and the wind blew so fiercely that photography became impossible, and hours when her movements would all

be standing silent in a row, according to dominance hierarchy, their backs toward a clump of high bushes which offered some protection from the wind. At such times it was almost certain that One Eye would be found eating nearby. She did rest, but it seemed that most of her time was spent grazing, which reemphasized the pregnant mare's need to provide nourishment for herself and for the foal she is carrying.

The mare in 98, stretched out on the ground, ready to give birth, raises a hind leg in an effort to force out the foal. If she had been closer to the herd at this moment, she would probably have attracted the attention of several colts and fillies, staring at and surprised by her unusual behavior. In 97 the foal is shown shortly after his head broke through the sac of membrane that still covers the rest of his body. His hind legs remain inside the mare. Twenty minutes later, the foal slides completely free from his mother as she gets to her feet (99). Of the hundreds of mares who gave birth in the fields where I was working, this was one of the few who foaled during the day. In 101 the mare has turned to sniff at her new offspring, who, ten minutes later (102), tries to get to his feet. Once up, mares usually start to graze and completely ignore their newly born offspring. Finally able to stand (103), the foal has a hard time keeping his balance as his mother continues feeding. While twins are scarce in most herds, Hope Ryden writes that they were not uncommon in the Prior Mountain mustang harems that she was studying.

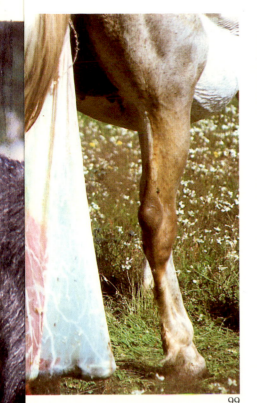

99

100

101

103

A newborn foal in 106 is approached by its older sister, causing the mother to extend her neck and flatten her ears in a mild threat. During their first hours, foals are extremely fragile and defenseless against the hooves of other herd members. Family stallions are generally protective toward their newborn offspring and stay close by mares who have just given birth. Seemingly more bored than irritated, the stallion simply moves away if the foal tries to nurse from him or bumps into him. In 107 the foal touches noses with its sister to establish a relationship that may last for years.

The mysterious disappearance or death of Camargue foals at Tour du Valat was caused, I felt, by the unusual situation of three family units living practically side by side. In a completely free situation this cohabitation would not exist, and foals would be safe from stallions other than their fathers. The disappearance of one of the foals, thought to be the offspring of the lead stallion, Darius, I would have attributed to bad luck. The remaining two foals were fathered by H-1, an aggressive young stallion with a two-mare harem. When I was at Tour du Valat, both of H-1's mares were in heat and he was constantly having to move them away from Darius, who literally stalked the threesome, and from H-4, a young gray stallion. Witnessing this, I thought that if one of H-1's mares had been foaling and was discovered by either Darius or H-4, a scuffle might well have resulted between the stallions during which a foal would accidentally have been trampled.

A week after I left the Camargue, Patrick telephoned to say that One Eye had foaled and that the stallions had taken no notice of her. Shortly after the birth, though, Darius' old mare (the dominant female) was seen to kick twice—maybe an accident—at One Eye's foal; once knocking it to the ground and another time into a ditch full of water. It is a natural reaction for a mare to kick at a strange foal that approaches her hindquarters. In Spain I have seen mares attack young foals with their teeth as well as with their hooves.

A mare's maternal drive is strong; wild females who have lost their young have been reported to try to steal foals from other harems or from mares of their own herds. Hope Ryden writes of having seen this happen and also of having watched a female who had lost her foal suckling another mare's baby.

THE FOAL

Foals pass their first few days nursing, exercising their legs, becoming acquainted with everything around them and sleeping. Periods of rest can last from twenty minutes to an hour. Once on their feet Andalusian foals suckle several times an hour. These nursing periods usually last three or four minutes. (Most foals continue to feed from their mothers until they are a year old.) When a mare is approached by her hungry foal she generally relaxes a rear hind leg, or takes a step forward with her front feet without moving the back ones which facilitate suckling. Climate obviously influences the foal's behavior. A three-day-old foal I watched in the Camargue tried to nurse for as long as ten minutes at a time, and then stood trembling next to his mother. He was too cold to flop onto the ground, which was covered with snow and ice, and the strain on his legs from not being able to rest, as well as the freezing air, caused him to shake. When he slipped and fell in the mud during a downpour that lasted all afternoon, and was being urged on by his mother and by gentle nickers and nuzzling from the herd stallion, I wondered how such a fragile creature could survive those conditions.

Almost without fail a foal shares the hierarchical positions of its mother when in close proximity to her. The offspring of high-ranking mares seem privileged with their dams' positions in the herd, just as the foals of subordinate females are generally low on the social totem pole in relation to their contemporaries. Age, as well as certain genetically inherited characteristics, such as size, strength and an active, aggressive temperament, are also influential. Even though the foals of low-ranking mares might be larger and stronger than their contemporaries, it sometimes seemed almost impossible for them to obtain a higher rank than their mother.

The foal in 108 is still half asleep; otherwise, being a very suspicious, apprehensive animal like its mother, it would have jumped up and run from the presence of the photographer. Neck outstretched, ears laid back, and mouth open in threat, the white mare in 109 warns a curious burro not to come any closer to her resting foal. When a foal rests, its mother generally feeds or dozes nearby (110). The foal in 111, left sleeping in the tall flowers by its grazing mother, is shown just as it arrives back at her side after moments of panic and a fast run. White flowers attract the foal in 112, who will taste them to see if they are good to eat.

109

110

111

112

93

113

114

115

Often a foal, for no apparent reason but joy in the activity, will suddenly start to gallop around and around its mother until even she has to lift her head and stare. After completing a number of loose circles, baby horses will often dash off across a field to find a gang of friends. The raising of the tail root is a sure sign of the wish to run, and once the foals were racing through Andalusian fields of flowers even some of the old mares would join them. Running is so contagious that if one horse starts, most nearby herd members join in. The photographs on this page show foals running—moments which are some of the most joyous to the horse.

116   117

T oward the end of the first month foals nurse less and nibble more at the grass. This nibbling, however, begins shortly after birth, for in their explorations of the world baby horses test all sorts of objects with their mouths, chewing and sucking branches as well as the hair of other horses. They also attempt to imitate their grazing mothers, an attitude which, because of their short necks, they can only assume with legs spread giraffe-fashion. In arid regions where foals have little nourishment but milk (which means that the suckling period is extended), some mares are reported to conceive every other year, thus giving their offspring a better chance of survival.

The foal in 116 quietly approaches a resting older sister, whose relaxed state is shown by her lowered head and laterally flapped ears. When the filly becomes aware of her brother's presence (117), she lays back her ears and tenses her muzzle in threat to discourage him from bothering her. The foal stands idly by for a few minutes and, once the filly relaxes again, starts chewing her mane (118). Some foals acquire a compulsive appetite for hair and, as adults, become a menace to horses with long manes and tails.

120

When only several days old most colt foals show an open interest in sex, often getting erections when smelling their mothers' genitals. Not much time passes before they start marking excrement with their own urine; occasionally they even flehmen, as the foal has just done in 119. The three-day-old foal in 120 stands resting with his dappled father and white mother. In six days' time, he, like the foals in 121 and 122, will be at his mother's side when she is in heat and is mounted by a stallion. The courting and copulation of horses in the free-living herd is an important part of a foal's education. Horses who have not grown up in a family unit are, like zoo-bred animals, often ineffective breeders.

Members of free-living herds watch with interest when a stallion covers one of the family mares. Excited foals even get underneath the mating horses or jump around them. Fillies also show curiosity, and young stallions occasionally become so excited that they masturbate, rubbing their penises against their bellies. Occasionally a domestic stallion will turn colt killer and, during breeding, nine- to eleven-day-old foals must be carefully guarded when their mothers are mated. This danger is rare among free-living horses though wild stallions have been reported to kill very young foals who were slowing down an escaping herd.

119

121

122

123

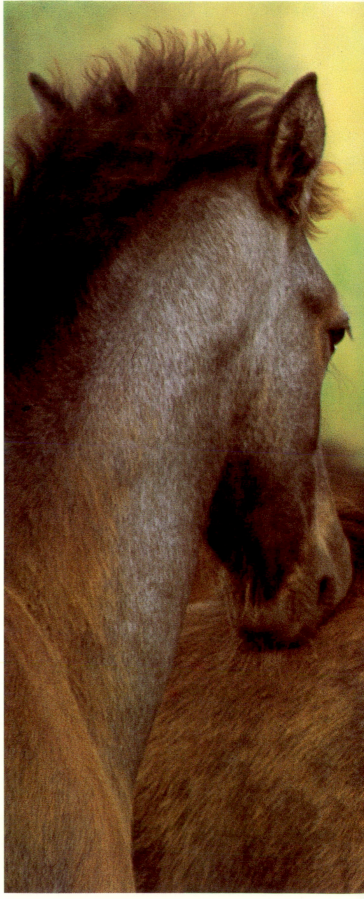

The foals in 123 and 125 are molting, as can be seen from their mottled coats. Friendships usually develop between young horses whose mothers spend time together, and often between foals of the same sex. Young fillies take part in running games but appear more subdued than males, who quite early begin to form their own gangs. The foals in 124 are engaged in mutual grooming; those in 125 are teasing one another, as can be seen from their mischievous looks—expressions that will eventually evolve into the facial signals used as threats in mock or real battle. Most play takes place in the cool hours of early morning or late afternoon.

124

126

127

128

A black foal initiates the game in 126 by approaching the bay and smelling his face. Suddenly the bay aggressively flattens his ears and rolls his eyes; the black foal momentarily signals neutrality, with relaxed eyes and ears in the lateral position (127). Then the black in his turn threatens the bay, who raises his head high in an attitude often used in play-fighting by subordinate immature bachelors (128). Most play-fighting involves mane gripping, the nipping of heads, rearing, mounting (usually from the side), tail biting, leg biting and chasing.

129

At the end of a play fight one foal will usually turn and run, the other in pursuit nipping at his rump. Both may stop to fight again or be joined by other members of the herd (129). Even older animals will be swept up in this exuberant game, which may take the form of follow-the-leader, the horses galloping single file in circles. Sometimes gangs of foals will engage in races (130), each trying to outdistance the other.

130

132

131

133

The Andalusian foal in 131 is four months old and trading his dark-brown coat for a gray one. Most Andalusian and Camargue horses are born black or dark brown, later changing to gray and eventually turning pure white.

Some foals (132) have close ties with their mothers; others do not. What is certain is that for their first year most filly foals are more closely attached to their dams than are colts. Unlike the colt shown in 133, however, who may not leave his mother until he is two years old, most fillies at the age of one become quite independent of their dams. Though mares seem to welcome and enjoy the companionship of their adolescent sons, they do not generally seem as friendly toward their weaned daughters. It appears, however, that young males never mate with their mothers; neither do family stallions cover their daughters. If mares in controlled herds maintain contact with their daughters, sometimes for life, in mustang family units stallions reportedly drive their female offspring from the harem once they have come into their first heat.

Like most young animals, foals learn both by trial and error and from watching

134

135

138

other herd members—they can be seen continually trying to imitate their mothers. Besides responding naturally to an itch, with teeth or hoof tip, most of the Arab and Andalusian foals in 134 to 139 have watched their dams engaged in similar self-grooming.

136

139

137

THE BACHELOR

140

HERD

Most colts, when they reach the age of three (sometimes a little younger or older), fall foul of the herd stallion and are driven from the family unit. Some extend their stay with the family by attaching themselves to a mare hostile to the dominant stallion, one who spends most of her time grazing some distance from the harem. Once a bachelor has been chased from his family, he usually quickly joins a herd of similarly dispossessed young males. Friendships between bachelors are among the strongest adult bonds in horse societies. Within bachelor gangs there is always a dominant animal who takes the place of the family stallion, driving his companions as if they were mares. Rank is most obvious at the dung pile, where each animal usually defecates according to his position in the hierarchy, starting with the most subordinate.

When two bachelor gangs meet, there is generally a fight. These skirmishes are not as serious as fights between family stallions, although, as shown on page 209, battles for the possession of favorite horses in the bachelor herd may lead to a certain amount of violence. Using a well-planned strategy, a gang of bachelors will often challenge a family stallion, but the younger horses are seldom successful in these confrontations. Until a horse is at least four years old he is generally not prepared to beat a family stallion in battle or to maintain a harem.

It is delightful to watch play fights among young stallions like these in 140, who often rear up against one another as if in slow motion, in contrast to the swift, serious combat of mature horses.

The colts in 141, with mischievous expressions on their faces, are preparing for a mock fight, which may have started with mutual grooming. If this were the case, one of the colts probably decided that he had spent enough time cleaning hair with his teeth, and took a hard nip at the other's skin. Teasing goes on continually between bachelors, a group of whom is shown in 142. Most biting is directed at the flanks, the rump and at the tender flexor muscles of the hind legs (hamstring bites are very common). The neck (143) is also a favorite target, and once a harassed animal is on the move his tormentors will continue pulling at his mane.

141

144

145

The stallions in 144, having been returned to pasture shaved and trimmed from a show, appear like black and muscled Nubian warriors engaged in a wrestling match. As they rear up against one another the subordinate stallion on the right, hesitantly raising a foreleg, shows his discomfort with ears and eyes. In 145 he holds his head high, eyes opened wide, now clasping the shoulders of his playfully nipping attacker. This action takes place so slowly and the horses remain on their hind legs for so long that they seem almost to be dancing. Leaning backward as far as he can, to try to keep from being bitten, the subordinate horse (146) clutches his partner tightly to avoid being pushed over.

147 148

When young stallions drop slowly back to the ground (147), the subordinate one will usually flee, the other nipping at him in pursuit (148). Once this chase stops, as in 149, the horses may calmly start mutual grooming, or, as shown in 150, begin pushing at one another with their heads, necks and shoulders, shoving, dodging and feinting, each trying to bite the other's forelegs, neck, shoulders and flanks. Often at this moment they begin circling round and round, head to tail, each trying to bite the enemy's hind legs. The number of circles usually ranges from four to ten, but I once counted twenty-four turns as two bays whirled in the dust. Surprisingly enough, not only did they keep their balance but they renewed their circling for a further ten turns in the opposite direction. Finally, when the play gets too rough, the subordinate horse rears, squealing (151), and the dominant animal then chases the loser (152) while biting at his flank.

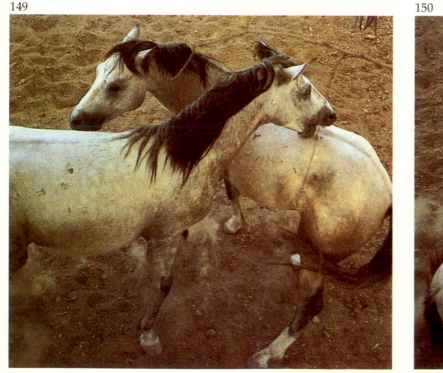

149 150

151

152

117

153

154   155

If the fight has not ended, the subordinate horse will halt, at which time more pushing and nipping take place before both animals drop to their knees to resume the game on a more serious level, like the chestnut and the roan stallion in 153. As both horses bite at each other's tender knees (154), another roan horse interferes to disrupt the play. The roan then chases and nips at the bay (155), who throws a play kick. In 156 a bay is seen in pursuit of a chestnut that he has been teasing. When one horse has had enough he may stop and kick out angrily at his pursuer. If both stallions decide to call it quits they may start to groom one another or walk off in opposite directions. Play fights provide young males with the exercise and the battle techniques they will one day need when, trying to steal mares, they confront tough old family stallions.

Since juvenile bands of horses now and then include animals of both sexes, it would appear that, apart from fillies forced out of harems by their fathers, some

mares are seduced from established family units by the joint efforts of two or more bachelors. The odds are great against one young stallion abducting a mare single-handed; it is more likely that one bachelor engages the family stallion in battle while his companion dashes into the harem to try to steal a mare. These mixed groups of young animals probably live relatively peacefully together until age forces one stallion to prove his dominance and drive off the other young males. He is then left with his own harem. The need to dominate seems to be the male horse's strongest drive—maybe actually stronger than sex—and for that reason he maintains a herd even during the long fall and winter months, when mares are not in heat. This hunger to dominate is best illustrated in the bachelor herd where the lead stallion, although he does not have sex with his subordinates, directs, drives and harasses them exactly as if they were females.

PERCEPTION

The horses in 157 are displaying one of the most basic equine characteristics—curiosity. What makes horses so obviously curious? Probably insecurity and fear. During the first few days spent with any of the wild or semi-wild herds I photographed, the animals reacted to me in a number of ways. If I was in a tree or hidden from them and their ears and noses had detected the presence of man, they would come to the alert position but would not run until they could see me.

Twice during my first days with a marsh herd, the lead stallion, probably more curious than aggressive, made mild charges in my direction—I was unfamiliar to him. Once a stallion from another herd ran toward me, ears laid back, eyes flared, neck outstretched and teeth bared. These threats and the curiosity displayed by other herd members ceased once the animals realized I presented no threat.

& CURIOSITY

157

With their acute sight, hearing and smell, horses are well equipped to investigate possible danger, although they rely mainly on their extraordinary vision. Unlike predators, who depend largely on their ability to judge distance in order to
capture prey, horses, because of their wide-set eyes, are handicapped by having to
rely mostly on monocular vision. Their binocular vision extends only over 60–70
degrees. While this may make them insecure in measuring space relationships, it
gives them an extremely wide field of vision and their ability to perceive slight
movement at great distance is outstanding.

The retina of the horse's eye is nonelastic, which affords an unusual method of
focusing. The bottom part is much nearer the lens than the top part. For free-living
horses this is a particularly advantageous arrangement, since while they are grazing

with their heads down both the grass before them and the horizon are in focus. When their heads are up, a slight raising or lowering of the head is used for focusing.

Equines are not only able to see colors but they also have extremely good night vision. The structure of their eyes closely resembles that of nocturnal animals, and in the many hours that I spent in the field after dark, I saw no difference in the horses' behavior, except in the case of foaling, which almost always takes place after sunset. The animals carried on their activities—including fighting, threat displays, and mating—with the same frequency as they did during the day. Some of those nocturnal observations were made with the aid of a light intensifier, which on a cloudy night provided a field of brightness much stronger than that given by a full moon. It was when I realized that the horse's nocturnal activities do not vary from those in the day that, for the first time, I felt some uneasiness in the field. The animals could see well at night and I could not, and when spending time with a set of stallions where there was frequent displaying and serious fighting, I began to feel insecure. This apprehension was heightened one night when, following a violent encounter between two dominant males, one of them, while trying to drive off his enemy, seemed to sense my presence and charged straight for me, veering off only when I raised my arms and shouted. More than a direct attack, I feared being accidentally knocked down and kicked. I reassured myself, however, that the possibilities of being accidentally trampled were slight, for although on a moonless night I could not see the stallions until they were only a few feet away, they could presumably see me.

Because the domestic horse often behaves in an exasperatingly stupid fashion, the inexperienced observer may take him for a completely stupid animal. On the contrary, the horse is also a very canny creature, and the two facets of his character make him somewhat of an enigma. Naturally, in equines as in people, individual capacity can vary greatly. Experiences with domestic horses had made me doubt equine intelligence in general—as well as their perception. But observing horses at liberty has done away with those doubts.

158

159

160

161

123

162

163

164

165

Darius, the Camargue stallion, often rested with a trancelike expression on his face, but little movement or activity escaped him. After a number of hours of observing wild family units, I came to admire the cunning, alertness and acute perception of the lead stallions. Often I watched as Darius stalked another stallion, H-1, who had two mares, both in heat. At first it seemed that Darius grazed toward H-1 and his harem by accident, but after a few days it became obvious that each move was cunningly calculated. What at first deceives the human observer of such carefully planned strategy is that the horse makes his moves while grazing head down, his eyes seemingly fixed on the grass. In fact, the horse's special vision allows him simultaneously to focus on both feed and distant objects. After realizing the craftiness with which Darius acted, I now and then had the eerie feeling that as he stood some distance away, resting in an apparent trance, he was watching my every move.

What special perception allows a stampeding herd to avoid the obstacles that may lie in its path? Granted, the lead animal can see these obstacles, but what of those horses in the middle of the herd? Some probably follow the actions of animals directly in front of them. Once I left my camera bag in a dry stream bed while I climbed a tree to locate a herd. Inside that bag were four expensive, uninsured lenses and two camera bodies with motor drives. No sooner was I in the top of the tree, scanning the hills, than I heard the rumbling of hooves, and before I could get to the ground, almost two hundred horses, in a cloud of blinding dust, came stampeding down the stream bed. I could only look at the bag—in the middle of their path—and grit my teeth. Once the herd had passed and the dust was settling, I climbed from the tree to find the bag untouched.

Equine vision, hearing and sense of smell are so much keener than man's that I, as the herd did, learned to depend on the ear and muzzle positions of the animals I watched to locate intruders or other family groups using the same home ranges. The horse's ability to rotate his ears independently of each other (163 and 164) is a great advantage in detecting sound. The large diameter of the ear orifice and the size of the outer ear allow a sense of hearing far more acute than we could ever dream of having. Often as I watched wild horses come to the alert position, all facing in one direction, obviously depending on sound or smell, since trees or brush obstructed vision, I would turn to the same direction and cup my hands behind my ears, only then being able to detect sounds that my ears unaided could not have captured.

Although it seemed that the horses I studied depended mostly on vision and hearing to detect threat, olfaction was also used for this purpose. Equines are probably equipped with a much keener sense of smell than they are normally thought to have. Although olfaction is more obvious in stallions than in mares it is equally important to both sexes. In confrontations and display rituals between males, the smelling of each other's nostrils and breath and especially of the lower flank often seemed to determine dominance. Only when a proper scientific analysis of the flank skin of stallions can be made may the true importance of flank sniffing be revealed. The stallion continually uses his nose to locate harem members, to sniff out messages from dung piles, and to test the excreta of mares for fertility. All horses use their noses when greeting one another, touching nostrils while sniffing noisily.

The creatures sharing the horse's home range are important sentinels for the wild herd. The cattle egret in 162 took wing once it detected me, warning the dozing mare. Egrets also become alarmed if the horse they accompany assumes the alert position.

One other capacity that in the horse seems extraordinary is its homing ability. Experiments have been made showing that animals, after having been released in a strange place, are able to find their way home, probably depending largely on the wind and their sense of smell. Horses separated by great distances from their herd have been known to go from dung pile to dung pile—and even to sniff at hoof prints—attempting to trace the trail taken by their companions.

Gorillas pound their chests in threat, cobras spread their hoods, chimpanzees beat the ground with branches, and geese extend their necks and hiss. The horse too has a well-defined series of gestures, ranging from the mild to the serious, which are used to warn and threaten.

Primarily reserved to maintain individual distance among group members, the most common warnings employed by equines are bite and kick threats. In family units these gestures are used mainly by harem members who are in continual contact with one another, and to a lesser degree by stallions who spend most of their time on the perimeter of the group, herding and watching for danger. In the mild bite threat, the most frequent warning, the aggressive horse flattens its ears against the top of its neck and swings its head and neck toward the intruding horse, mouth open, lips tightened to expose both incisor and canine teeth. If the warning is more serious these motions will be accompanied by a lunge—possibly ending with the bite itself.

When a horse employs the kick threat it turns its rump toward the threatened horse, raising one hind leg slightly off the ground. At the same moment the tail may also be swished angrily, while the animal moves backward a step or two. If this does not produce the desired response, the kick will then be delivered with either one or both rear hooves.

THREAT

166

DISPLAY

B ite and kick threats are most commonly used by nonreceptive mares to discourage stallions, by females protecting their young, and by group members not in the mood to tolerate close contact (about a yard and a half) at water holes and dusting sites.

Stallion threat displays are much more pronounced and interesting; they range from eye rolling (page 134) to posturing, driving, the foreleg kick (also used by mares), and finally to the direct run. The direct run, which is used to move family members or to chase away intruders, is illustrated in 166, with the stallion stretched out in full gallop, ears back and neck extended. The foreleg kick is often seen in stallion displays, and is accomplished by striking out at the enemy with one or both front legs.

The gray in 167, swinging her head high, is responding to a kick threat from a bay, who is swishing her tail and cocking a right leg. Warning the photographer, the dark stallion (168) circles, prancing, tossing his head and rolling his eyes. The white stallion in 169 threatens while at the same time seeking escape from an uncomfortable situation; he rears slightly while laying back his ears. The strange position of his mouth is not normally associated with threat warning.

A good example of the bite threat is shown in 170, as a white mare attacks a subordinate who signals peaceful intentions with her raised head and ears.

169

168

172

173

A more serious bite threat, accompanied by a lunge, is being used by the young stallion in 171 as he claims possession of a dusting spot. The roan mare in 172 is employing a threat gesture with which I was often greeted. This consists of staring at the intruder while rolling the eyes, ears laid back as the head is tossed up and down several times in succession. In 173 a gray mare issues a mild threat, flapping her ears angrily while she swings her neck and swishes her tail.

The white stallion in 174 is assuming the driving threat attitude to aid him in moving his harem. His flattened ears, gooselike outstretched neck and head, and slightly raised tail warn harem members that if they do not wish to be bitten they had better move as directed. If a stallion assumes the driving attitude and walks toward mares, they respond by walking away. If he runs at them, they react rapidly. The closeness of the stallion's head to the ground, the exaggeration of his overall body attitude, and the speed with which he is moving determine the strength of the warnings. A very low-held head signals extreme threat. Dominant males who also wobble their heads from side to side in a snakelike movement are usually highly possessive of their harems and spend more time herding and keeping tabs on mares than do more easygoing stallions. The intensity of driving depends on the character of the individual horse and upon the situation with which he is confronted.

174

The turning of the eye in its socket until only the white and the under edges are showing is an elementary part of a stallion's repertoire of warnings. This rolling of the eye, which can be accompanied by head swinging and exaggerated and impressive posturing, does not appear to have been previously recorded, possibly because it happens very rapidly and is overshadowed by more obvious and distracting gestures. Some stallions roll their eyes more than others. One family leader at the King Ranch (177 through 183) so exaggerated his eye rolling and posturing that the first time I saw him display I had the feeling I was not watching a real horse at all, but some fiery mythological steed.

Eye rolling, because it takes place so quickly, was only apparent when the photographs I took of stallions were finally developed. Having to use a fast shutter speed to minimize the movement of a large telephoto lens, I often shot at one thousandth of a second, and was surprised to see that the developed transparencies showed very exaggerated and constant eye rolling in excited stallions. In bachelor herds, for some reason, stallions who had covered mares rolled their eyes more than did virgin males, perhaps because they had already sampled sex and, desiring more, were easily excited. In 175, during a play fight the gray leader of a bachelor gang rears above a subordinate and rolls his eyes until only the white and the very red edges show. The tight downward curve at the edges of his mouth also signals aggression.

EYE

175

ROLLING

DANGER

A dominant family stallion usually tries to re- move his harem from the presence of danger. Where there is no alternative, he will challenge the intruder. If the stallion, such as the horse in 176, is unsure of the threat he may leave his harem and investigate.

A mature, angry stallion is an extremely dangerous and frightening animal. I spent four years in Spain photographing fighting bulls and I had a number of very close calls, some so close that I feared for my life. Years of selective breeding of the Spanish bull have created one of the most deadly animals in the world. However, after a few encounters with angry stallions, if the choice had to be made, I'd take my chances with a bull.

On a number of occasions when I encountered a family leader for the first time, he would threaten me by posturing, much as if I were a male horse. If the intruder was another stallion, a number of devices were used by a dominant family male to avoid physical violence. Of these, threat displays, mock battle and dung-pile rituals were the most common. Some stallions put on more elaborate displays than others.

177

178

The gray in 177 is worried about the proximity of another stallion and steps forward to investigate. Because the white mare near him is in heat and because the intruder maintains his distance, the gray seems to have decided to display instead of leaving his harem to issue a challenge. In 178 he tosses his head high, rolls his eyes and swishes his tail. While the white mare assumes the sawhorse position (179), the stallion continues to swing his head, gesturing with his mouth, whose edges curve downward in strain.

In 180 the stallion, completely involved in the display, purses his lips and puts even more exaggeration into his gesturing. The white mare, seemingly bored by the whole business, steps forward in an attempt to capture the gray's attention. While the stallion escalates his display, the mare (181) stands by patiently. In 182 the mare again spreads her legs in the sawhorse position but the stallion is still too intent on threatening the intruder to notice her. When the intruder finally retreats the gray stallion assumes the driving attitude (183) and begins to herd his mares. The horse pictured on these pages was abnormally exaggerated in his threat display. Unpredictable and aggressive, he more than once attacked riders and their mounts who ventured too close to the harem. While working on an earlier book I often found myself having to escape threatening stallions who progressively cut terrain while circling me.

180

182

181

183

141

SUBMIS

184

W hen one horse walks away from another's threat, this is submission. A mare not in heat kick-threatens a stallion—the stallion walks away. He submits. A filly comes too close to a resting foal and receives a bite threat from the foal's dam—the filly submits and moves away.

The most interesting signal of submission I witnessed, teeth clapping, was not always in response to threat, and it was used by most young horses such as the filly in 184, who demonstrates her inferiority by stretching out her neck and raising her head toward the gray stallion's head. The filly's mouth is open and her lips are drawn to expose the incisor teeth, while the lower jaw is moved up and down. She also tucks her tail and draws in her hindquarters possibly to try to appear smaller.

The youngest foal I saw teeth-clap is shown in 185. He is demonstrating his inferiority to one of the dominant females in an all-mare herd. Although teeth clapping to dominant mares was seen in family units, this submissive gesture was generally directed by juvenile males toward the dominant stallions.

SION

After unsuccessfully attempting to mount a mare, the white horse in 186 starts to graze and is approached by a teeth-clapping youngster. Having displayed at a dung pile, the stallion in 187 has his domination acknowledged by the submissive behavior of a gray colt. Following a fight with another harem leader, the dominant stallion in 188 is seen walking back through his herd. Each colt he passed acknowledged him with teeth clapping.

While some investigators feel that teeth clapping is an expression of ritualized grooming, my observations indicate that it is a purely submissive act that allows young horses to express their subordination (like rump presenting among baboons), thus probably avoiding frequent aggression from older, stronger stallions. Since most teeth clapping was directed toward a dominant horse after he had displayed, fought, or had a negative encounter with a mare, it also illustrates just how observant horses are of the behavior of other animals in the herd. Only by exhibiting such obvious submission, especially at moments of excitement in the herd, are immature animals tolerated and now and then safe from attacks such as the one on this colt in 189.

Another possible form of submissive behavior, rump presenting, which was observed in a bachelor herd, is described on page 150.

Hope Ryden once saw a fight between four members of a mustang bachelor gang and a very aggressive, powerful stallion. At one stage in the fight the dominant horse directed his attack against a yearling. Once the young animal had been thrown to the ground, it maintained its submissive posture while mouthfuls of hair were torn from its mane by the stallion. At this point the other bachelors joined the enemy and turned on their fallen companion, ripping at his mane in what appeared to be the typical turncoat behavior often found in species which follow a pecking order. Blood, however, was not drawn—hair pulling seemed a symbolical substitute for real biting. The yearling's submissive attitude appeared to have saved him from being maimed or killed.

Once the yearling was allowed to get to his feet, the fight continued and the old stallion quickly chased off the remaining bachelors. He then returned to the yearling, assumed the driving position, and herded the young horse toward the harem as if it had been a newly captured filly rather than a colt.

185

188

186

189

187

FRIENDS

190

HIP

PLAY

195

196

197

In a bachelor group friends often engage in activity that seems more like tag or follow-the-leader than fight play. On the morning that I took the photographs on these pages I saw some bachelor behavior I had not seen before.

When six yearlings who had spent a week at the Jerez Fair were returned to the herd there was much posturing, running, flank sniffing and play-fighting, while the hierarchy of the herd was redefined. Once this initial excitement was over, I saw a handsome bay two-year-old approach and present his rump to the gray lead stallion. At first I took this for only a mild kick threat by the bay. After the gray had smelled the younger stallion's lower flank, genitals and tail root, the bay did playfully and mildly kick out his back legs, in what seemed an attempt to arouse the stallion's attention more and to excite him, before running off a short distance with the dominant male in pursuit. The stallions stopped fifty yards from the grazing herd, where the bay once more deliberately presented his rump to the gray several times in succession in the same apparent weak kick threat. It was done submissively in much the same way as young baboons present themselves to high-ranking males in a clear demonstration of dominance hierarchy.

That day and the next I noticed similar behavior among dominant stallions and subordinates. Why didn't the younger horses teeth-clap to show inferiority? Why hasn't rump presenting in horses been mentioned by other observers? Was what I was watching purely play-kicking, purely rump presenting or a combination of both?

199

198

The rump in 195 belongs to a colt who, for the third time in succession, is backing it into a dominant friend. Seemingly having succeeded in reestablishing his friendship with the older horse, the colt responds (196) to a nip from the stallion by turning his head. With renewed confidence the colt bit teasingly at his friend, after which he prances off (197) with the stallion in pursuit. Stopping (198), the colt rears slightly and playfully bites at the older horse's lips. The stallion nips, causing the colt to roll his eyes and play-threaten with his ears. While the colt's forelegs clutch out at his friend, the stallion's relaxed eyes and upright ears show that he is enjoying the game. In 199 the stallion, front hooves off the ground, hangs his neck over the slightly startled colt's withers, causing the younger animal to brace himself under the weight.

In play games, colts often half rear from the side to tangle their forelegs over their partner's neck or back, perhaps trying to force their opponent to the ground.

200

201

202

203

WEATHER

Horses are hyperconscious of weather fluctuations, which have a remarkable effect on their behavior. Air movement, temperature and humidity are factors which govern most herd activity.

On sultry days the animals were quieter than when the weather was mild (204). Just before a storm, when there is great atmospheric tension and the air is highly charged with ions, almost all the horses appeared nervous, restless and aggressive. When I was doing a study on the fighting bull, the influence of thunderstorms on animals was even more obvious. In one pasture I remember watching some five or six pairs of bulls all engaged in fights triggered by atmospheric tension—fights that sometimes end in death. In stormy weather there was also increased fighting among stallions in bachelor herds, and horses of both sexes became hyperactive eaters, slowing down once the storm had broken. Strong winds also stimulated activity— fight games and running, as shown in 200. Even before leaving home on a windy day I knew good camera material would be waiting in the country.

During August in Andalusia and in the western United States, where the temperature regularly rises to over 100° F., most horses doze from late morning until late afternoon, when, as in 203, they resume grazing. When snow and ice cover the marsh (202), the herd must spend more time feeding, pawing at the earth to uncover the sparse winter vegetation and to loosen roots. Wind and rain have become too uncomfortable for the herd members in 201, who have sought the protection of a stand of high brush. Backs to the wind, each of these animals has positioned himself according to the hierarchy of the herd, with the very subordinate animals on the fringes—the least protected areas—of the group. The head of the white lead stallion can be seen raised slightly higher than the heads of the other horses.

DOZING

The horses in 205 through 208 stand in the typical dozing position, ears relaxed and laterally drooping, lower lip hanging, necks straight out or down, front legs together, croups down, and one back leg cocked at an angle with only the hoof-tip touching the ground. Adult horses spend more time dozing than they do in either of their other two forms of sleep: resting, in which the animal drops to the ground with its legs positioned beneath its body; and deep sleep, where the horse lies stretched out on its side. In fact, apart from eating, more of a horse's life (except for dominant stallions) is spent dozing than doing anything else. It is in this attitude that the animal appears least attractive—even a fine stallion when he is dozing will not seem very handsome to most people.

REST

TING

DEEP SLEEP

216

The foal in 215 was sleeping so soundly I could have touched him and he would not have awakened. To prepare for this third and deepest form of relaxation, horses roll completely onto their side from the huddling position, as is the white mare in 217. They then stretch their head, neck, and body flat out on the ground, as a mare being bothered by her hungry foal is doing in 216. During deep sleep, which usually takes place at night unless the ground is very wet, horses are almost completely unconscious. Some observers have reported that when wild herds rest, one or two sentinels always remain standing, ready to alert the herd to sudden danger.

When foals are very young, like the one in 218, they literally throw themselves onto the grass and fall asleep immediately with their mother grazing, dozing or resting nearby. If a foal awakens and its mother is not in sight, terrified, it begins neighing and running until it sees her or hears her short, guttural call. All the foals I watched rested or relaxed in deep sleep except for a sick filly who dozed. Some sick adult horses will not lie down—they seem to fear being unable to get up in case of danger.

The horses I photographed would not rest or sleep just anywhere. They had special places, and while most of them had favorite trees under which they dozed, deep sleep always took place with the animals stretched out in the open, where the wind's messages could reach them. Apart from choosing areas that offered the security of the open, the mares' only other bedding preference seemed to be for dry ground.

The distance horses keep from each other while grazing is generally respected while resting. For example, one ancient white mare, who seemed to enjoy her solitary life, grazed far from the herd and also stayed away from the others when she slept. Related mares and their foals can often be seen sleeping close together, occasionally even touching one another. At one ranch in Spain, finding the sleeping herd in the early morning, I felt as though I had come across a bloodless battlefield with horses' bodies flung out flat and still in all directions. Sleeping habits obviously depend much upon the circumstances in which individual herds are living. If horses are constantly exposed to danger, they can seldom indulge in the security of deep sleep.

Seconds before 219 was taken, this gray mare was sleeping so soundly that when I touched her lightly she didn't awaken. Breathing loudly and snoring, something most horses do in deep sleep, she had probably also been dreaming—moaning and groaning, twitching her eyelids and ears and now and then a leg. Patrick Duncan told me that he thinks horses dream, and that males sometimes have erotic

220

dreams. Several times he has observed the dominant Camargue stallion, breathing loudly and vocalizing in deep sleep, awaken suddenly, spring to its feet and try to mount the nearest mare.

When I touched a hoof of the mare in 219 she gradually began awakening, through various stages of consciousness. First her breathing changed, becoming forceful and louder. A minute passed before her ears showed more pronounced movement, her eyes opened; and a few seconds later I took this photograph as she lifted her head, stared at me through half-opened lids, then let her head drop back to the ground. Less than thirty seconds later the message that something was not right reached her. Then like the mare in 220 she raised her neck and head, rolled to the resting position, straightened her forelegs and jumped to her feet.

The stallion in 221, having been roused from sleep by the warning snort of another horse, leaps to his feet to face the intruder. Never having been caught off guard by me before and seemingly embarrassed, he then rushed forward aggressively, posturing to reestablish his domination of the photographer.

Many horses live their entire lives without being able to stretch out on the ground to enjoy deep sleep—their only form of relaxation is dozing. The combined resting periods for most adult horses observed—dozing, resting and deep sleep—averaged about six to eight hours a day.

219

221

abit is probably not as important in the lives of horses as well-worn paths might indicate. Although in mild weather and in a secure situation a herd may seem to have fixed hours for resting, grazing, and for traveling each day the same trail to water, this regularity is ended with even slight fluctuations in the weather or by environmental changes.

The horses in 222 can be seen running single file along well-worn paths cleared of vegetation by constant use. The use of these paths probably did not depend so much on habit as on the ease of traveling established trails instead of wasting energy having to break new paths through even low vegetation. A second factor influencing the single-file use of paths in 222, 223 and 224, and having nothing to do with dominance hierarchy or group leadership, was the sharp thistles growing on these hillsides. The mares' tender lower front legs received less punishment if one horse followed another.

Synchronized herd activity is often mistakenly associated with habit. The first time one witnesses this phenomenon one cannot help but be impressed. I remember watching three family units grazing when suddenly, as if someone had flicked a switch, they stopped eating, and within a short time all twenty-two animals were dozing. Once the resting periods ended, it seemed that the switch was flicked back and the entire herd, as if on command, started to graze. Synchronization occurs only when the whole herd is at ease. The sole pattern that it seems to follow is that many herds, two hours before dawn, can be found dozing, resting or snoring away in deep sleep.

222

223

224

HABIT

226

Horses devote many hours to self-grooming, and practically all the herds observed had favorite dusting spots. Although at times horses roll on grass (225), the dust bath is essential: removing excess oil from the animal's skin helps to order matted hair in its natural direction. Herds living in the marshes of southern Spain tend to prefer mud to dust baths, probably because mud protects them better against insects and also, when it dries and falls off, it removes dead hair and skin.

When a harem reaches a dusting spot the mares usually roll first, followed by the dominant stallion. If it is a bachelor group, again the leader generally rolls last, subordinates taking first turn in another expression of dominance hierarchy. Colts and stallions usually roll more than fillies and mares.

On arriving at a dusting site, a horse will lower its head, ears forward, to smell the ground, pawing at the earth as the stallion in 226 is doing. After this formality, the horse, taking short steps, will generally circle the chosen spot several times before lying down. It is not easy for equines to lower themselves to the ground, for unlike meat eaters they do not have very flexible vertebral columns. To get down for a bath, a horse normally collects his four legs under his body, then, bending at an angle so sharp the muscles vibrate with tension until they will no longer hold his weight, he drops onto his forelegs and rolls over on his side. Clumsy, old or pregnant mares sometimes let themselves practically fall to the ground.

227

228

229

A large bachelor herd (227) has just arrived at a dusting spot, where a subordinate gray is first to lower himself to the ground while other members of the herd squabble over bathing rights. Most aggressive is the bay stallion (behind the standing dapple gray), who charges with ears laid back, determined to keep the retreating dark horse (upper left) from bathing. In 228, while the gray continues to roll, several other horses have their attention attracted by another gang of bachelors out of camera range to the right. The subordinate gray continues to groom himself in 229, while the bay once again attacks the dark horse, who, in a clear expression of the pecking order, now threatens the subordinate horse next to him. In 230, another gray member of the same herd is next to roll, not allowing the quarreling of the other bachelors to disturb his bath.

230

231

232

233

234

H orses, like the mare in 234, may use their teeth to groom shoulders or forelegs while they are dusting. Generally, however, like the pink-muzzled stallion in 231, they first press their heads and necks to the earth to scratch their flat sides, especially their cheek regions. After dusting and scratching one side of their bodies most horses will roll to the ungroomed side. Some animals repeat this process several times. Other horses will rise from the flat-out position to the huddling or sitting position (232), hind legs partly under their bodies, forelegs extended to loosen the soil in preparation for another roll. Old and pregnant mares who cannot or do not want to roll over completely get to their feet after having dusted one side, lowering themselves back to the ground to dust the other side.

Once risen from his bath, a horse will shake vigorously, like the stallion in 233, to cover himself in a haze of dust. In 235 a mare dirties her white coat but gets a satisfying grooming by rolling in slightly dried mud. The stallion in 236 had been traveling this muddy trail on a freezing winter day when the dominant male of another family stopped fifty yards up the path to roll. The horse in this photograph also lowered himself to the ground and is shown just getting to his feet. From the two bands, consisting of more than twenty horses, only the dominant males paused to take mud baths.

235

236

237

238

Usually, dusting is so infectious that once one horse has started to roll, the other animals follow suit. If the bathing area is large, several animals will self-groom at the same time. If it is small and the herd is all female, dominant mares dust first. A horse's need to care for its hair and skin by baths of dust or mud is so great that when a stabled horse is put into a corral where there is damp or dry earth, his first action, when he feels secure, is to drop to the ground and roll.

Horses use their teeth and the tips of their hind hooves for self-grooming (134 through 139); they also use tree trunks, branches and large rocks. The gray mare in 239 is scratching her back on a low branch so slowly that every moment seems to savor of delight. In 237 the white stallion is vigorously tossing his head up and down to relieve an itchy neck. A slower scratch is enjoyed by the mare in 238.

240

241

Water is irresistible to some horses and even on a cold day these animals, like the black mare pictured here, will not pass up the chance to bathe. Entering the water, the mare paws at it, splashing her head and chest (240), after which she lowers herself into the pond (241), rolling on one side (242), then the other. She exposes her teeth and flashes her eyes in an expression of pleasure (244). To stand she assumes the resting position, and in 245 is in the process of extending a foreleg. Upon emerging from water an equine spreads its legs sawhorse fashion for stability, and then what first starts out as a headshake travels all along the body to the root of its tail.

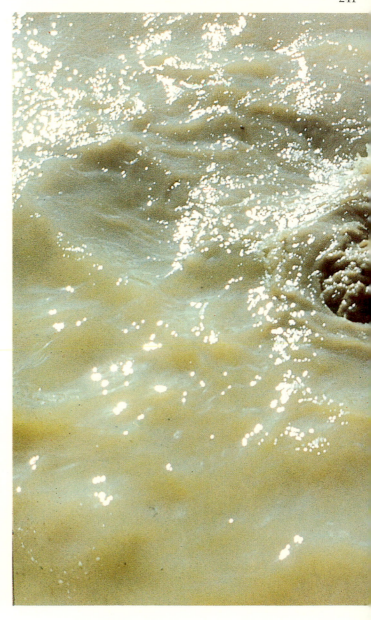

245

242

243

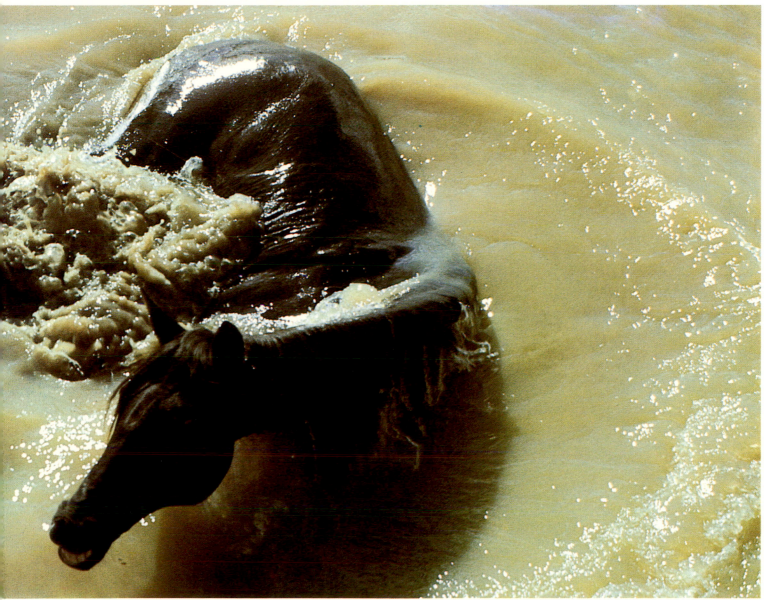

244

MUTUAL GR

OOMING

248

247

The Przewalski's mares in 246 are shown in what is probably one of the most common means of social and physical interaction among horses—mutual grooming. When this activity is initiated, a passive animal is usually approached from the half front by the horse who desires to initiate grooming; in 247, however, the interested gray mare makes her approach from the rear. The animal that wants to groom, with a subtle facial expression that can clearly be read as "Let's scratch backs," advances or retreats, depending on the ear, eye and body response of the horse it is propositioning. If, as in the case of the Przewalski's mares, a proposition has been accepted, the animals will first smell each other's nose and neck, or stand together for a few minutes, after which they position themselves next to one another, head to tail, and start biting in short, firm bites at each other's neck, as the grays are doing in 248. If this action is intense, the sound of their teeth is clearly audible as they start on the mane crest, pulling at hair (249) and dead skin. Seldom is grooming not a mutual effort (250). Slowly working along necks, withers and backs, the horse usually stops grooming at the tail roots (251)—one of the most satisfying places to be scratched if you're a horse. Average mutual grooming time is only a couple of minutes, though it can last five times as long. If one animal stops, the other generally also stops. When finished, horses usually stand together, head to tail, for a short while, grazing or dozing, or change sides to resume grooming. Not only does this activity allow animals to scratch parts of their bodies that are unreachable with their own mouths, but it also probably serves to form friendships and to strengthen the social contact that is so important to the wild herd.

This form of grooming generally involves only horses in couples, although I have seen three mares or bachelors simultaneously scratching one another's back. Only rarely is a dominant stallion seen grooming another horse, and in these instances his partner is most often a young mare in heat or a young male. In some cases a threat from a stallion might cause a colt to initiate grooming in an attempt to appease the older horse.

251

249

250

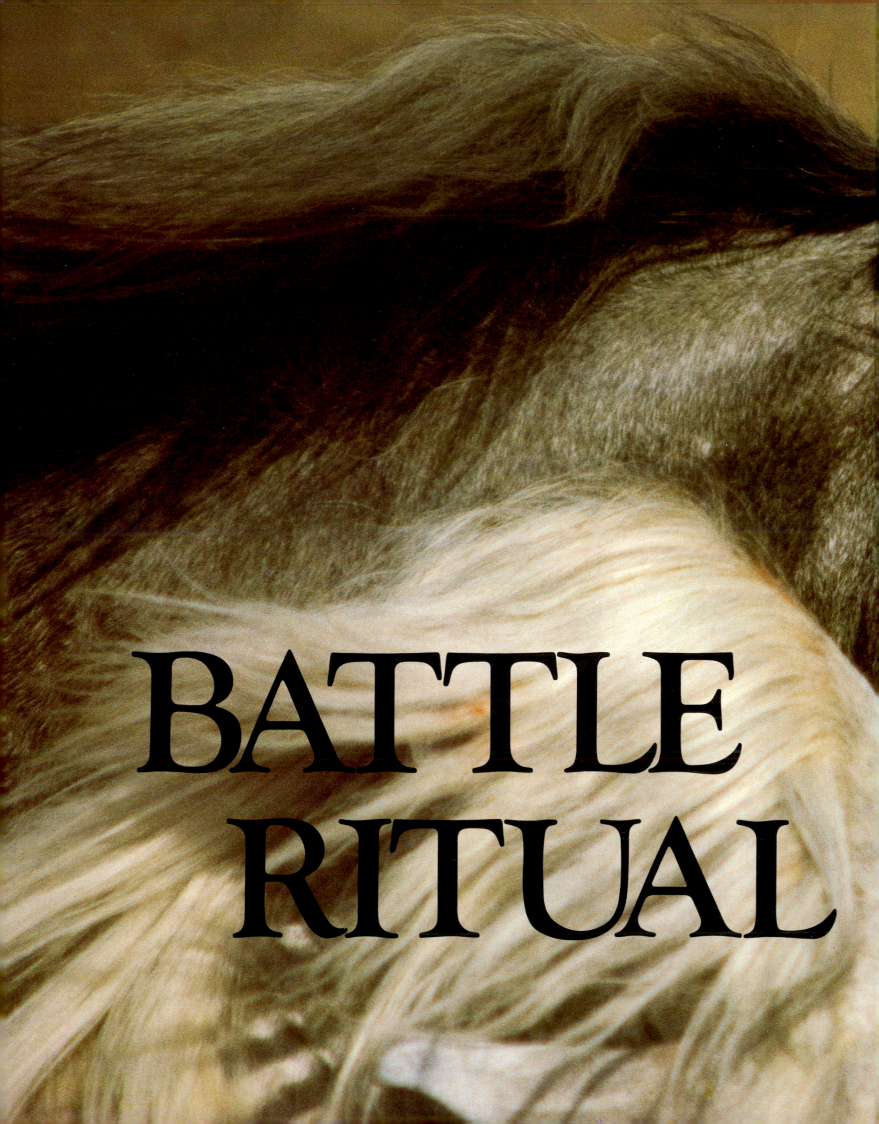

BATTLE RITUAL

262

260

263

261

Circling head to tail (260), the horses begin their battle by biting at each other's sensitive rear leg tendons.

In 261 two stallions momentarily break physical contact to display in a parallel prance. Parallel prancing is often followed by further fighting. In 262 the white and the gray commence biting at one another's forelegs and neck—first blood has been drawn by the gray, who in 263 clamps his teeth into his posturing opponent's mane crest.

They also push with their shoulders and strike at each other with their heads and necks in a combination of posturing and fighting, which shows that they are not only unfamiliar with one another but are also young and inexperienced, factors which will keep their fight relatively mild.

264

265

266

267

In 264 both horses rear, the gray biting at the white's high-held face. Separating briefly in 265, the stallions once more seek to impress each other by posturing and rolling their eyes. The gray then rears, while his opponent rolls his eyes, tucks in his chin and arches his neck (266). Chin tucking, apart from serving to protect the throat against another stallion's bite (the jugular being a prime target), also makes a stallion's neck even more arched and impressive and is an important part of displays such as the parallel prance. The white (267) suddenly decides to bite the neck of the gray. In 268 the gray, still on the offensive, lunges and retaliates.

Once the white stallion decided he had had enough he turned, kicked out weakly with his hind legs, and was chased off by the gray.

RETURN O

F A LEADER

POSSES

SION

The hyperactive gray stallion in 311 was the leader of a bachelor herd, and the only horse in his gang who had covered a mare. The behavior of this older, sexually experienced stallion was completely different from that of the calmer male virgins around him. Not long after joining the herd, he claimed a black stallion for his companion—perhaps the dark horse was the same color as the mare he had covered. From that moment, the sexually aware gray jealously guarded his virgin friend. In part this companionship became a real torture for the black, for he was never left alone, always being nipped at, hurried on and herded by his suitor; on the other hand, it meant that he enjoyed a high place in the herd hierarchy. Since sexually experienced stallions are hyperaggressive and hyperactive animals, they are nearly always the high-ranking males in bachelor herds. This means that their partners, when in close proximity, like foals of dominant mares, can do as they want, having the security that the animal who "loves" them will protect them. Prime spots are thus assured at resting, dusting, feeding and watering places.

312

The gray leader in 311 is in a dangerous mood. A strange stallion has arrived on the scene and threatens to steal some of the younger gang members, among them the black. In 312 he and the dark-gray intruder both signal aggression with laid-back ears and arched necks; each stallion also threatens with a raised foreleg. As the challenger moves in from the left in 313, the light gray rushes forward to separate him from a bay. Using a half rear buck (314), the leader threat-gestures to discourage the dark stallion (still almost out of the frame to the left) from collecting a bay and a chestnut colt, both of whom, having suffered under the light gray's rule, would need little encouragement to abandon him. While the challenger, ears back, stands by in 315, the leader, using the most extreme of threat signals, tries to keep him from the younger bachelors.

313

314

315

335

336

As the stallions rise parallel to one another in 335, Darius, who has been punished most, gets a good bite at H-1. Although the animals were rearing and appearing to try and bite at one another, it seemed that there were moments during these battles in which for some reason a kind of truce existed that called for both stallions to go through the motions of combat without the infliction of physical harm. Each horse is aware that if his kicks and bites become too vicious, the enemy will respond accordingly—and neither really wants to get hurt. In 336 scars of previous fights are visible on the back of H-1 (on the right). He also bears on his neck mud scrapes from Darius' hooves. This is a very dangerous moment for Darius (on the right in 337). Stretched almost to his full height, his balance uncertain, his position is made even more precarious by his forelegs, which are reaching upward and cannot help to stabilize him. Also, the larger stallion, H-1, on the left, is lunging as he pushes forward. If a horse is thrown over backward his chances of injury are great, for he is then at the mercy of his enemy.

337

According to Patrick Duncan, in the study of horses at Tour du Valat, observers had never seen a stallion topple another in combat and then attack him on the ground. Good luck allowed me to photograph this action on my first morning in the Camargue. The battle that preceded the series of photographs reproduced here was almost a repeat of the fight depicted in 328 through 337. The younger and stronger but subordinate stallion, H-1, had finally reared up against dominant Darius, who in

stretching himself as tall as he could was pushed off balance and thrown over backward. The action lasted no more than ten seconds.

In 338, as Darius hits the ground, H-1 plunges in on top of him, striking down with both forefeet, his mouth open to bite. In spite of the excitement of battle I was intrigued by the subtlety with which the mares disguised their interest in the fight. However, once Darius was on the ground, the group of females to camera left

339

341

340

342

started to show a little life. Even though Darius lashes out with his teeth and hind legs (339) to defend himself, still he has no chance against H-1, who, in 340, sinks his teeth into the dominant stallion's neck. In 341, as H-1 gets a better grip on Darius' throat and straddles him with his legs, the fallen stallion screams with pain. In 342 Darius has managed somehow to roll over and get his legs underneath his body, frantically attempting to regain his footing, though now completely defenseless against H-1.

Once Darius was on his feet the fight ended and each stallion joined his mares. Most battles do finish in draws, both stallions simultaneously returning to their respective harems. Why didn't the seemingly victorious H-1 continue fighting? I am sure that he was as surprised as Darius when the dominant horse was thrown over backward. Phil Malkas and Peter Paalvast, who also saw this battle, agreed that, apart from being smaller and easier to push over than his opponent, Darius had probably slipped in the muddy ground around the dung pile where the battle started. Prone, helpless and humbled, Darius bore little resemblance to the horse who for years had dominated H-1. After H-1's victory tension was high, and for the next few days the stallions often reared up against one another, but Darius remained dominant.

In the months that followed my work in the Camargue, I often thought of Darius. One could not help but admire him. When Claudia Feh visited Sevilla last summer she told me that she also shared those feelings for the "little, big stallion." His life was not easy, having to keep H-1 and H-4 in line and having to be continually on guard for attacks from the G-4 stallions or from members of the bachelor gang.

The last time I saw him was very early on a freezing misty morning. High in a tree I was shaking with cold wondering what I was doing at such an hour in such a place under such miserable conditions when nearby one of Darius' mares suddenly came to the alert position. Several other horses then also assumed the same position. Whatever had attracted them was on the far side of a stand of tall brush. Facing in the same direction as the mares, I cupped my hands out behind my ears to pick up sounds of more than one horse moving through shallow water.

Then from behind me came a stallion's snort. It was Darius, head high, ears forward, trotting through the low scrub. What horses, moving through water, out of view, had attracted him? The G herd with its trio of aggressive stallions? The bachelor gang, looking for a fight and mares? I raised the camera and focused it on Darius as he gathered speed and moved forward to investigate.

EPILOGUE

Many of the photographs and observations would not have appeared in this book had I not been able to study horses at Tour du Valat, a private wildlife reserve in southern France founded by Dr. Luc Hoffman. Spreading out over five thousand acres of the Camargue, this naturalist's paradise is somewhat reminiscent of parts of the Coto Doñana in southern Spain. Of the many projects at Tour du Valat which study wetland ecosystems, one concerns the ecology and social behavior of horses.

When the study began in January 1974, the herd consisted of fourteen animals—one mature and three immature stallions, seven mature and three immature mares. Though the herd has been almost constantly under observation by the study group, it has been little influenced by man. To the Tour du Valat horses, man is an inoffensive animal similar to the rabbits and boar which also roam the 840-acre home range. If a young horse curiously sniffs at a human investigator, the human moves away from the animal. Older horses show practically no interest at all in the people around them, which makes for an ideal, and probably unique, study situation.

In December 1974, when an older horse, Darius, was introduced to the herd, one of the young males left the band within twenty-four hours.

By August 1975 Darius had chased another three-year-old stallion from the main herd. The three-year-old joined G-2 to form the bachelor herd.

In January 1976 the main herd consisted of twenty-seven animals: the dominant stallion, Darius, and six other sexually mature males; twelve mature and seven immature females. During that year, however, Darius chased seven young males and one immature female from the main herd. Of these young stallions one was later killed accidentally while fighting for possession of the filly.

Nineteen seventy-seven was a year of action at Tour du Valat. Three members of the bachelor gang (G-4, H-1 and H-4) returned to the main herd to fight intensively with Darius for several days, with the result that one of the bachelors, G-4, began the nucleus of a new band by driving a mare (H-2) and her yearling (K-4) from the main herd. By the end of the year the G band had grown to thirteen animals. These were either animals stolen from Darius, bachelors who had managed to attach themselves to it, or young females who had joined of their own accord. Although G-4 tried to keep the bachelors from joining his family group, two young males did so. The remaining three members of the gang were successfully driven off.

At the same time two bachelors, H-1 and H-4, were somehow able to attach themselves to one of Darius' old mares and during the subsequent months they were gradually able to reintegrate themselves into the main herd.

By the beginning of 1978 Darius possessed only three adult mares; H-1 had two and H-4 had rather weak links with two. When I arrived in the Camargue in February of that year, the main herd consisted of twenty-seven animals (comprising three family groups), the G herd of thirteen, and the bachelor herd of three sexually mature males.

Why the stallions H-1 and H-4 had chosen to stay with Darius and the main herd is not clear. Why had Darius allowed them to remain? Perhaps because after forty-eight hours of trying to drive them away, he was simply unable to do so. Some of the study group felt that links were so strong among mares of the main herd that the two young stallions were unable to drive females from the company of sisters, mothers and friends. I would attribute this unusual situation to the limited size of the fenced home range, which even though large was not so big or unrestricted as to give security to the young stallions H-1 and H-4. If they did set out on their own with a harem, they ran the risk of being attacked by the mature male members of the G herd or of having to take on the bachelor gang single-handed, and probably losing mares. Darius, even though he was also a threat, had for the moment anyway allowed H-1 and H-4 to keep their mares within the main herd; and since he has always been dominant at Tour du Valat, he offered some protection and security, especially against the bachelor herd. On the other hand, by allowing the two young males and their mares to remain with him, Darius could count on them when the bachelor group decided to attack, which it did with some frequency. If the home range had been larger and unfenced, H-1 and H-4 might have struck out on their own.

This unique situation provided an extraordinary opportunity for the study of the social behavior of horses, for while H-1 and H-4 and their harems formed part of

ACKNOWLEDGMENTS

The opportunity to study equines in several countries was in part made possible because of assistance from Greg Garrison, a man whose passion in life is horses. Apart from Mr. Garrison's interest in equines in general, he is involved in a personal project that could one day be responsible for helping to preserve one of the world's rarest and handsomest breeds—the Andalusian.

While I was working on a previous book, *Equus,* I lived day after day in Southern Spain with herds of purebred Spanish horses, and with each look through my camera I realized why they have inspired more artists than have any other breed of horse. Their thick necks, muscled chests, finely sculpted heads, long manes and tails, noble dispositions, spirited temperaments, and natural, high showy movement make them one of the most artistically exciting animals in the world. For those who might be skeptical about the Andalusian's appeal, I refer to the Spanish horse on the cover of this book and to the one pictured on the opposite page. Andalusian blood runs in many of the world's equines, from the Mustangs of Montana to the Lippizzaners of Vienna.

As my field work in Southern Spain drew to a close, reports from Portugal were disturbing. Political changes there had led to violence, and a number of purebred Lusitano mares and stallions (a breed almost identical to the Andalusian) were said to have been slaughtered by peasants. Other herds of the finest Lusitanos were being broken up as landowners tried to sell their property and get money out of the country. Since Spain was about to also undergo political change, it seemed quite possible that the Andalusian might one day be in similar danger.

This apprehension, however, was done away with when I learned that the Garrison Ranch at Thousand Oaks, California, has assembled a breeding herd of pure Andalusians as large as any in Spain. And not only has Garrison gathered such a sizable number of animals, but he has been able to collect mares of the purest strain along with the International Champion, Legionario III, a stallion whose blood lines can be traced back almost five hundred years. Legionario is considered to be one of the finest Andalusian sires in the world, based on confirmation and breeding. It was comforting to know that Andalusians have been safely established in the United States. Greg Garrison's efforts might be compared with those of another American who also loved horses. During World War II, General George Patton had moved the Austrian Lippizzaner herd from the path of the advancing Russians and into safety behind American Lines, a strategy that was vital to the survival of the Spanish Riding School of Vienna. The author expresses his gratitude to Mr. Garrison not only for his assistance with this book, but also for his dedication to this noble breed of horse.

In Spain the following ranchers and their foremen have my thanks for help with this project: Juan Manuel Urquijo Novales and his foreman Antonio Garamendi Márquez; Antonio Romero Girón and his foreman Juan Aguilar Herrera; Francisco Lazo Díaz and his foreman Antonio Sánchez Carrasco; Jesus Terry Merello and his foreman Sebastián García Nieto; Miguel Angel Cárdenas Osuna; the Marques of Salvatierra, his son Rafael Atienza Medina and their stud director Francisco Montaño Galán and foreman Manuel Cervera Camarero. Michael Hughes and Bob Adams were also of great help at the King Ranch's Spanish property. Luis Ramos Paul was kind enough to read the manuscript.

Work at the Spanish military ranches would not have been possible had it not been for General Pedro Merry Gordon. At those ranches I would like to thank Colonel Eduardo Pérez Ceresal, Colonel Antonio Doce López, Captain Antonio Ribarda González, NCO Antonio Sola Castillo, NCO Alfonso Cañero Muñoz, and recruits "El Sevillano," "El Granadino," and "El Rubio."

Spanish veterinarians who helped me gain access to ranches near Sevilla and Jerez were Antonio Méndez Benegassi and Francisco Abad Alfaro. Félix Moreno de la Cova, Agricultural Delegate for Andalusia was also helpful in making contacts. For observations of marsh horses and work done at the Coto Doñana Reserve, I thank its director Javier Castroviejo.

In France Dr. Luc Hoffman has my deepest appreciation for allowing me to visit and photograph at Tour du Valat where I was assisted by the horse study program director and my good friend, Dr. Patrick Duncan, as well as by the horse study group: Claudia Feh, Phil Malkas, and Peter Paalvast who also have my gratitude for having read the manuscript for this book.

In the United States I thank Greg Garrison and Budd Boetticher for allowing me to photograph their horses. The San Diego Wild Animal Park at Escondido, California, and its staff also provided me with valuable assistance, as did James A. Michener who traced for me the evolution of the horse at the Denver Museum.

For editing the manuscript of this book I am deeply grateful to Matthew Robinson. Rudolf Blanckenstein, friend and printer, kept my spirits up as did my agent Gloria Loomis, as well as Howard Cady, my editor at William Morrow. Elias García and his staff at Cromoarte have my thanks for the excellent job they did with the color reproductions as does the staff of Imprenta Sevillana for their care with printing and binding.

John Fulton I thank for the long hours he spent on the book's design. And to my assistant José Franco Cadena I am grateful for his continued enthusiasm.

The film used for all of the photographs was Ektachrome X forced developed to ASA 160. Cameras used were two Nikon Fs equipped with motor drives, a 50-300 Nikkor zoom lens and a 28mm wide angle lens.